The Peril in *Thinking and other essays*

I0420482

JOHN WOODCOCK

D EDICATION

To my mother (I had to call her "Mother") who inadvertently catapulted me into precocious knowledge of the cold, alien realm of *thinking*, and to her sister Pat, who gave me the warmth and love that kept me human.

C ONTENTS

ACKNOWLEDGMENTS

Cover graphic: Wanderer Above the Sea of Fog by Caspar David Friedrich (1174-1840)—a prominent German Romantic poet. The painting was a favorite of Heidegger's. Cover design by author. All graphics are in the public domain.

PREFACE

My short, pithy title, The Peril in *Thinking*, as it stands, is open to much misinterpretation, and it would be better said as The Peril "in" *Thinking*. To clear the way immediately, I am not advocating a cessation of thinking, in favor of feeling or irrationality. I am not offering a moral argument against thinking. I am not referring only to ordinary language as a means to communicate established meanings to one another. My quarry lies elsewhere, and my method is phenomenological. I will offer two quotes to "set the stage". The first is from classicist scholar, Karl Kerènyi:

> For the great mystery which remains a mystery even after all our discussing and explaining, is this: the appearance of a speaking figure, the very embodiment as it were in a human-divine form of clear articulated, play related and therefore enchanting, language—its appearance in that deep primordial darkness where one expects only animal muteness, wordless silence, or cries of pleasure and pain.[1]

This one is from Parmenidian scholar, Peter Kingsley:

> Perhaps you noticed it out of the corner of your eye —how even the most seemingly ordinary events can sometimes have such significance that slip right through our awareness. And sometimes things can come to light, discoveries are made, that literally make no sense ... The situation could be compared to thunder and lightning out in the countryside, so intense they can't be seen or heard: invisible lightning, silent thunder. Our minds simply won't acknowledge what's happened. And it's not only that everything seems to go on exactly as it did before; we're not even conscious of anything happening. But there, where our awareness doesn't yet want to reach—that's where the future lies.[2]

To reach this living quality of language, where language is a *happening*, as Heidegger says, we must cross a threshold, from what I call, after Owen Barfield, the plane of ordinary consciousness to that of extraordinary consciousness. These two planes are not separate realms of experience, with a literal threshold. They are co-extensive, or simultaneous, and both lie as "within" us, or *as* our "within-ness".

Our culture in the West has privileged the plane of ordinary consciousness to the extent that we have lost touch with the plane of visionary experience or "inspiration" altogether. Yet, whenever our Western culture undergoes the upheavals of a transformation or paradigm shift, there seems to have been an inceptive moment where the plane of living language appears or breaks through to certain individuals, who are then given the task of bringing new language back across the threshold into the plane of ordinary consciousness through some kind of art form (which obviously includes the art of writing). We are now in such a time once more, and many individuals are, in one way or another, making contact with this threshold. This is where the peril lies.[3]

Modern psychology seems to have an increasingly dominant view that the "cause" of most, if not all by now, mental illnesses, lies in a childhood trauma of one kind or another—psychic trauma or literal abuse! This theoretical split of course originates in Freud's seduction theory. In my view, more and more people are turning up "traumatized" because "something" is breaking into the ordinary plane of consciousness from the plane of extraordinary consciousness and it is doing so through the "opening" provided by any weakness in the personality—a weakness that appears in the imagination as "the wounded child or animal." As Leonard Cohen says, there is a crack in everything and that's where the light gets in.[4]

Or lightning!

Today the psychic background to our existence is an upheaval of self-transformational movement. Because our cultural practices and epistemology in general today have no knowledge, or even interest in this "background reality", these upheavals are "breaking in" with the violence of a thunderstorm. Alternatively, many individuals, who sense the presence of such a "creative" ground, are reaching for its treasures purely on the basis of self-interest, with no ritual preparation. The result is that living language is "breaking into" the ordinary plane of consciousness as the hidden "within-ness" of our daily discourses, and is determining events in the world. We apprehend and literalize this incarnation as untrammelled power operating in many domains of human interest, most notably politics, economics, and the media. In its most extreme form we recognize it as totalitarianism and fascism—two major political forces that shaped the 20th century.

My essay points to an even greater peril than these, for the peril lies now within the *language* of our ordinary plane of existence. We have usurped a *being* greater than ourselves and brought it willy-nilly into the domain of ordinary existence, where its self-transformational *telos* has perverted into ideological outcomes, operating throughout our daily discourses.

Four others follow this title essay, each concerned, one way or another with the mysterious relationship between language and being, or with how the contours of our world are constituted in and through language. This is also the mystery of psyche and world.

I wrote Drought or, The Wasteland, as a submission to "DROUGHTaction"–a Panel & Online Community Conversation–Sept. 22, 2015. I wrote Psyche in Oblivion around 2009 (originally titled Newspeak), in response to a TIME magazine issue dedicated to Mind & Body (2007). Participatory Consciousness was written in 1998, as part of my doctoral work. Tarning is a long essay, concerned with the subtle incarnation of new meaning in language, and is drawn from my book, Manifesting Possible Futures: towards a new genre of literature, 2013.

End Notes are included at the end of each essay.

---

[1] Kerenyi, K. *Hermes: Guide of Souls*. Dallas. Spring Publications Inc., 1990, 88.

[2] Kingsley, P. *In the Dark Places of Wisdom*. London. Duckworth, 1999, 228.

[3] See: Woodcock, J. C. *Overcoming Solidity: World Crisis and the New Nature*. Bloomington. iUniverse, 2013.

[4] From his song, "Anthem".

THE PERIL IN *THINKING*

Language is the danger of all dangers because it first creates the possibility of danger. Danger is the threat that beings pose to being itself. Danger thus means that we forget being because of the prevalence of beings. Language is the most dangerous good because language appears to address beings and beings only. The problem is precisely that language discloses beings as beings and we, of course, need that disclosure as we necessarily are in the world. But at the same time this disclosure of beings covers over *beyng*.

Martin Heidegger

INTRODUCTION

This essay is concerned with thinking, more specifically, living language, and I want to demonstrate what I mean by starting with fossilised language, the kind of language that we use daily to successfully communicate established meanings. Such language may even be called institutionalised language, as in "established for some extrinsic purpose," like education, public service, government, etc. The focus is usually not on the language itself but on its external references in the empirical world. What happens if I shift my focus for a moment from the obvious empirical references of the word "institution" to the word itself? One way to do that is by appealing to the dictionary and its institutionalised meanings.

I noticed immediately that "institution" is paired with "establishment" quite frequently and both words have this interesting morpheme, *sta*, which suggests a root meaning, and indeed there is one—*stā*. Both words spring from this etymological root, as do many others. There is an image held in this meaning: to stand, an ancient example of which is a stallion, or studhorse standing. So often words in their modern, dried, desiccated, abstract usage spring from a "past" that is alive, vital, concrete, and of the sensual world. As I looked more deeply into this root-image I was struck by the plethora of word meanings that spring from it. They occupy a full column of my very large AHD! But my imagination was particularly drawn to a few words that stood out for me—understand, thread (from "stāmen"), epistemology, and most startlingly, ecstasy. Who would have thought that ecstasy and institutions have anything to do with each other? As we will see in my essay to follow, these words appear frequently. They belong together as aspects of a deeper meaning that wants to "presence" itself through my writing: the meaning of a stallion standing—a very alive, generative image indeed, and perhaps already we can already begin to see how ecstasy and institutions belong together in the image of the horse, if we remember the winged horse Pegasus who struck a rock with his hoof and released the waters of poetic inspiration.

At present a dark spirit is working its will in the world through many institutions, wreaking terrible damage on the lives of human beings. I am not referring primarily to external events in the empirical world. I am speaking of language, or the being of language. There is a darkness within language itself, i.e. our modern language, through its various manifestations as emotions, perceptions, images and finally, thought, or thinking.

As I descend into this darkness and bring you, my reader along, and if I remain faithful to the movement of language itself, then it seems that, when the darkness reaches its nadir, we may encounter the generative downward strike, lightning-like, of a horse's hoof, from which a flood of new language will emerge—*poesis*, the unknown future!

This, then, is a story of the journey towards discovery —the discovery of what it takes today to remain what I am and always have been, one ordinary human being, at a time when a non-human being, or way of being, has succeeded in seizing the human spirit and, so far, is appropriating the generative downward strike to its own ghastly ends—manifesting as totalitarianism!

Back Story

I arrived in India in the middle of the night. The moon was full and I could easily see that there was nothing familiar in the vegetation surrounding the airport in Delhi. A friendly stranger warned me not to pay more than thirty rupees for the taxi into Delhi. I decided to linger for a while at the terminal, to drink in the humid air, filled as it was with strange odours, and to settle my mind for the next phase of my journey. I was soon soaked to the skin through my thin shirt. I had read how hot India is but now I was beginning to feel it. As the crowds thinned out, I noticed a few glances in my direction from dark faces. I wasn't behaving in the expected manner of tourists, who mostly get bundled off quickly as possible to the supposed safety of some familiar westernised hotel.

After a while, tired as I was from my flight, I grew even wearier of the barrage of demands from the remaining taxi drivers, and finally succumbed to one who yelled the magic words into my dripping face: thirty, or "t'irty" rupee. I was eventually going to get used to the new spatial proximity required for conversation in India, but now it felt oppressive, over-bearing, aggressive— none of which feelings, I learned later, belong to the moods of India. I was simply reacting, in a typically Western manner, to an entirely new cultural context.

As we headed out from the airport, in the open rickshaw, the horizon opened out to a wide moonlit plain with palm trees silhouetted against the sky. A long winding narrow road threaded through the grassland and at its end I could see the lights of New Delhi slowly emerging into focus. Now that the driver had secured his fare, he concentrated on driving and soon the high whine of the two-stroke engine, with its foul emissions of smoke and oil, receded into the background. I sat back and sank into the somewhat eerie atmosphere of this old, old land.

As the ensuing days reached into weeks, India slowly and silently drew me deeper into its spell. My initial angry reactions to the constant press of people reached a peak one day on a bus to Srinagar—and transformed! The bus was filled with young Muslim men and I had become a matter of interest to them. At the time, Pakistan and India were fighting over their border in Kashmir and a division had opened up, once again, between Muslims and Hindus. The young men on the bus were apparently engaged in heated (it could have been normal for them, of course) debate, when my neighbour suddenly turned towards me and loudly demanded, in quite good English, "what do you think about Kashmir?"

All eyes turned towards me. It was those dark eyes, somehow darker even than the dark skin of their faces, that captured me. My fear rose to a crescendo and then suddenly dissipated. These were not eyes of hostility. Passion, yes, and there was an innocence in them that has long gone in the West. These eyes were not assaulting me. They were wide open and taking me into their depths. There was nothing personal about this. They were reading me in a way very different from what I was used to. It was more like diving into a pool of considerable depth and silence. Those eyes were simply receiving me. I muttered something about not knowing enough to comment, was rewarded with a flurry of advice on what I should believe from now on, and then I was once again left alone on this crowded bus of Muslims.

From Kashmir I travelled to Dharamsala, in the foothills of the Himalayas. The bus took us further up the mountain road, in drenching rain, to McLeod Gange, the home of the exiled Tibetan government. During my three-week stay there, I visited one Dr. Dolma, physician to His Holiness. The waiting room was filled with local people, dressed in little more than rags, and as well, a very healthy population of fleas. One fellow eventually emerged from the shadows and gave me a bottle to pee in. I did so and the bottle then disappeared into another room. I was ushered in to a room where a large Tibetan woman sat. She lifted the bottle of urine in the air and swirled it, watching the bubbles carefully. Then she took my pulse and, from what I could feel in the pressure of her fingers, she was reading three different pulses. Finally she made her diagnosis, in Tibetan, and sent me out to get some pills—three different kinds. These pills were pure herbs, each prepared by rolling between the fingers into a dark concentrated ball, and then blessed by the breath of the doctor.

During this time in India, my soul life opened up and a plethora of dreams came through. Many incorporated the symbols I saw daily on my travels, in order to tell their story. They moved me so deeply I was even compelled, on one occasion, while in McLeod Gange, to visit a Rinpoche in order to ask him about it. I wanted to ask him if he could tell me about any serpent rituals, that being the theme of one particular dream. Through our translator, a young monk who wanted to practice his English, I learned that the serpent "needs to go into a pot" and that I should write a book.[1]

My descent into the spiritual life of India continued as the weeks went by but on one occasion, when I was in a hotel at the center of a very busy city, I received the shock of a dream that held the gift of the unknown future, or at least one thread of my as-yet-unknown future. It wrenched me out of the spiritual life of India back into my Western tradition.

It is dark, 3am. I am with a young woman and her son. She is knocking urgently at Dr. Dolma's door. Dolma gets up and stumbles around to turn on the light. The woman goes in and I follow. She is telling Dr. Dolma that, due to her treatment, the young boy's condition is beginning to reverse itself. His right eye had been dying. They sit down and she shows a picture that the boy drew when his condition began. He is in bed watching three flies transfixed to the wall by fly swatters. Smoke or a fog is in the foreground. He begins to claw at his eye. In my haste to understand, I take the picture before Dr. D has a chance. She takes it back, saying no, no, to me. She is in relationship to this woman and I disturbed it. I get angry and leave as both women go "tsk tsk". I am angry that I do not know how to heal like that. I just do not understand. Meanwhile, Dr. D tells the woman that her own expectations of her son have something to do with the problem. He is not as strong as she imagines. Sometimes the problem is simply 'mum'. Deal with that and the problem disappears.

When I woke up I drew my response to the boy's dream picture and this is what it looked like:

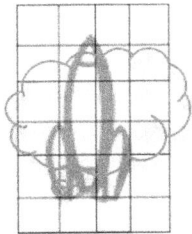 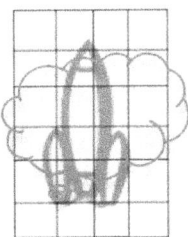 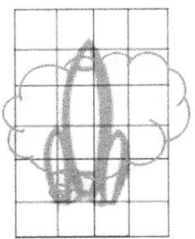

I could immediately see the crushed flies (there were three of them in a row in the dream picture) also as rockets and phallic symbols. But although the dream was replete with mysterious connections, the Cartesian grid lethally imposed on the living flies struck me most, at the time. There, in the middle of a bustling city of India, I wandered the streets looking for a bookstore that might have a copy of Descartes' Meditations. I found one. I was burning with a question given to me from this dream: how does a mathematical grid "freeze" or "fix" life, even destroy life? This was a new thought and it initiated a new direction for me, one that has gripped me for many years. Like the little boy, I had to understand!

My entry into the domain of Western thought and its relationship to life or *being* had begun.

Rockets & Cartesian Space

One focus of my subsequent research was the work of Wolfgang Giegerich, a psychologist in the Jungian tradition, who is also well versed in Continental philosophy. The combination of philosophy and soul psychology represented in his books challenged and excited me for many years. One essay in particular, when I first turned to it, immediately released a memory of my forgotten dream.[2] In this essay Giegerich opens up the archetypal foundations of what we take for granted today: empirical reality itself. He makes a psychological shift from the ordinary perception of rocket ships as empirical objects to soul perception of the "rocket ship" as image, i.e., our modern way of being that enables us to construct empirical rocket ships in the first place.

He shows how our modern empirical reality *and* what we call today fiction both had to emerge from a unitary form of reality that was logically prior—what he calls imaginal reality. Prior to the eruption of the logic of empirical reality, the foundation of imaginal reality was depth, what we might call today the infinite depths of soul, but what our ancestors simply called "world". In sharp contrast, the foundation of the empirical world is fixity, positive fact, the archetypal symbol being the Crucifixion. Giegerich goes on to show how this foundational principle of fixation is mathematised in the symbol of the zero and the Cartesian system of co-ordinates. This fixity of course leaves behind a corpse, the once-living cosmos!

Thanks to Giegerich's eye-opening and penetrating analysis of the archetypal foundation of our presently constituted world, I began to understand how a Cartesian grid might kill natural life, as my dream shows. Was this the little boy's problem in my dream? Was he scratching at his right eye because he couldn't see clearly (because of the fog), yet felt he needed to "get it"? With this thought I felt a deep resonance with the little boy's plight. As long as I can remember, my entry into the domain of thinking has been characterized by a gesture of anxious staring. I "had to get" whatever I was studying. [3]I felt there was something "at stake" in my drive to understand. I had to drive a stake into whatever I was studying, to fix it with certainty—and this intense and exhausting striving was backed by my gesture of anxious staring, trying to see things clearly. I wasn't so much trying to study this new domain of thinking. I was anxiously trying to think its manner of being—to become it! This meant that I was anxiously learning how to kill life in a missile-like manner, like fixing flies on a grid-like fly swatter, killing them in the process. All the while, something was dying—my capacity to see clearly, pictured in my dream as the fog and the little boy's dying right eye.

In the little boy's urgency to see clearly, i.e. to "get" this new way of thinking, or more radically, to become it, so destructive to life as it is, what is he not seeing? What is this "fog" in his way, and how is "mum" involved in his healing? He draws a picture of his plight. Is this a factor in his "healing", a different kind of seeing, perhaps?

The Fog of Life

My immersion in Continental philosophy broadened, thanks also to the work of other scholars. I eventually found my way to Heidegger and embarked on an intensive course of self-study for several years. I was not deterred by the serious charges of Nazism that have been levelled at Heidegger. After all, Jung had faced similar accusations and I still found his work to be of inestimable value. I felt I could also keep Heidegger's thought and his personal attitudes separate.

I was particularly attracted to his work represented in his pioneering book Contributions to Philosophy. In this collection of aphorisms, Heidegger is trying to feel his way into a kind of futural thinking, out of the customary present-indicative mood of traditional philosophy. I was sure this work could help me with my investigations of a new kind of literary genre that would be performative, in the sense of speaking a new way of being into existence, rather than speaking *about* this new way of being, thereby remaining in the current mode of empirical reality. I eagerly turned to an American interpreter, Richard Polt, who wrote a book on Heidegger's Contributions.[4] Polt examines this very question of the possibility of a future-indicative mood in philosophical thinking.

I was about two years into this particular study when I accidentally came across a YouTube audio replay of a talk Polt gave at a conference in 2014.[5] It was the title of his talk that delivered the first shock and "caused" my 1985 dream to erupt into consciousness again. The title is: Inception, Downfall, and the Broken World: Heidegger Above the Sea of Fog. "Fog"! What does philosophical thinking have to do with fogs? My dream shouted at me: there is a fog in front of the little boy's eye when he tries to see clearly, fixedly! I immediately spent several hours transcribing the lecture so that I could dwell with it slowly, taking it in. I knew that Polt's talk, and its central image of the fog, was crucial to the speech of my dream and the subsequent unfoldment of this thread of my life.

Polt's study of Heidegger's Black Notebooks leads him to conclude that:

> Heidegger comes across as a completely unempathetic and unimaginative individual. Openness to the other goes deeper than metaphysics or any worldview or any narrative about the fate of the globe … he not only has no sympathy for real suffering individuals but also thinks he knows them but he does not—the dismissive statements in the Notebooks, such as the repeated claim that he is living in the age of a total lack of questioning and thought. The fact is he does not know if others are questioning. … Although Heidegger left National Socialism altogether, he did not leave unscathed. He left wounded, poisoned, embittered. He did not get clear …[6]

Polt notes that a change overcame Heidegger between the 1920's and the 1930's when he seemed to lose all feeling for individual human beings and he (Polt) asks what could bring on this change in Heidegger's thought. He tellingly quotes a passage from the Black Notebooks that seems, in part, to account for this startling change in Heidegger:

> When Heidegger becomes Rector, he writes that he is acting for the first time against "my innermost voice" but once in the position he steels himself, reminds himself of his determination and fights all the harder as if determined to plunge into the opacity of errancy, what he calls in "Being and Truth," the difficult becoming of a dark future.[7]

Heidegger seems to be telling us here that in order to pursue his style of thinking he had to ruthlessly overcome his innermost voice—a voice that might warn him, perhaps? Something inhuman appeared to be taking him over and his chose to accept it, knowing full well the cost to his human essence, as he delved more deeply into Nazism, from which he did not emerge unscathed, but instead, "wounded, poisoned, embittered." Polt adds, "I do not think he ever managed to get in the clear. He was not fully clear about himself, or with others; nor was he clear about the world that he had chosen in 1930 to see from a particular *befogged* [my italics] point of view."

Polt amplifies his search for an account of the unsettling transformation in Heidegger's attitude from the 20's to the 30's—a transformation from relative empathy towards fellow human beings to an inhuman dismissal of empirical life altogether—by focusing on the complex of clarity and "befoggedness" in Heidegger. He refers to a painting from the German Romantic tradition that Heidegger praised in the Notebooks:

One of the Notebooks' little surprises is Heidegger's praise for the painter Friedrich. Heidegger must have known what is today Friedrich's most famous painting, The Wanderer Above the Sea of Fog. Heidegger must have felt that exhilaration from thinking of himself as one of the rare dwellers on the mountaintops. But I wonder whether he reflected on the mists. The wanderer in the painting has a magnificent view but he does not see all. The clouds obscure the valleys below. Maybe he doesn't care and maybe that's part of his triumphant mood. So be it but at least he should realize that he doesn't know what lies under the mists. The heights are both the heights of knowledge and ignorance. This is one reason that Zarathustra goes down and why the philosopher-kings must return to the cave.[8]

It seems that striving wilfully for the clarity of the heights, backed by a mood of exhilaration and triumph, or even ecstasy, constellates a compensatory image of the fog, or as I say, befoggedness. Clear knowledge and ignorance become strangely interchangeable. Polt wonders whether Heidegger reflected on the mists and, in my dream, the little boy's anxious striving to see, or better, to think understandingly what he sees on the wall, prevents him from seeing or attending to the fog that lies between him and the grid, except as an obstacle that brings on anxiety and blinding.

A contemporary parallel to Heidegger's complex surfaced in memory, as I contemplated the strange presencing of the fog right in the middle of where one would expect clarity and certainty—both in Heidegger and in my 1985 dream. In Memories, Dreams, Reflections, C. G. Jung reports a waking experience he had when he was only twelve years old:

> I was taking the long road to school … when suddenly
> for a single moment I had the overwhelming impression
> of having just emerged from a dense cloud. I knew all
> at once: now I am myself. It was as if there was a wall
> of mist were at my back and behind that wall there was
> not yet an "I". But at this moment, I came upon myself.
> Previously I had existed, too, but everything had merely
> happened to me. Now I happened to myself. Now I
> knew: I am myself now, now I exist. Previously I had
> been willed to do this or that; now I willed.[9]

Jung's remarkable experience demonstrates a strong
connection between wilful striving, clarity as an "optical"
kind of knowledge, and the equally sudden presence of
the fog that, in Jung's case, now appears "behind" him.
His entire childhood, as it were, is consigned to oblivion,
as is necessary for a move into psychological adulthood
(at least in modern times—the self-willed isolated
individual). In the painting that Heidegger was drawn to,
we can observe the same heroic and isolated figure,
standing on the mountaintop, overlooking the foggy
valleys below. This figure also seems to be related to the
"Siegfried" dream which appeared in Jung's later life, in
1913: "… [t]hen I heard Siegfried's horn sounding over
the mountains and I knew we had to kill him …". He
later concludes, after considerable guilty suffering over
the death of the golden hero:

> … suddenly the meaning of the dream dawned on me.
> "Why, that is the problem that is being played out in the
> world." Siegfried, I thought, represents what the
> Germans want to achieve, heroically to impose their
> will, have their own way. "Where there is a will, there is
> a way!" I had wanted to do the same. But now that was
> no longer possible. The dream showed that the attitude
> embodied by Siegfried no longer suited me. Therefore it

had to be killed. After the deed I felt an overpowering
compassion …[10]

A dream murder, particularly if the murder is committed
by the ego (even if accompanied by a non-egoic
companion, the "unknown brown-skinned man, a
savage") does not mean that is the end of the matter as
far as wilfulness goes (after all, how can we kill off a soul
quality when the very nature of soul is "formation,
transformation/the eternal Mind's eternal recreation")?
Jung in the dream is exercising the same will in the very
act of murder. "It had to be killed"—according to whom
—Jung's ego? Even if there were some deeper intent, as
embodied in the figure of his unknown companion, it is
simply that form of the will (the culture hero Siegfried)
that is dispatched. One consequence is that Jung's own
wilfulness can no longer be "seen" by him and therefore
is likely to go "underground", as indeed it did, in his
subsequent confrontation with the unconscious. The Red
Book is a record of a sustained continuation of that very
will, but now in relation to the inner world. It seems to
be a matter for the future to ask what would unfold in a
human life, if we instead follow the "overpowering
compassion" that is born in the heart, following the
"death" of the self-willed one. In the very least, Jung's
dream gives us the "unthinkable" thought that there is an
intimate connection between murder and the birth of
compassion.

As self-willed subjects, we rise above, or leave behind,
or discover as "between", something that has to do with
knowledge/ignorance, will/compassion, appearing as
"fog". We can go further back in our Western tradition to
find additional amplification of this cultural issue.

In the 15th century, an unknown monk wrote a guide to the contemplative life, called the Cloud of Unknowing. He valorises the transcendent god and in so doing, must negate the commonplace, ordinary empirical life, including the body:

> Given that speech is a bodily activity performed by the tongue, a bodily organ, it must always be spoken in bodily words, ... of the work that belongs to God alone I dare not take it upon me to speak with my blabbering fleshly tongue. ... Some people are so burdened with strange and foolish habits in their bodily conduct that when they hear something they twist their heads peculiarly to one side, and up go their chins. They let their mouths gape open, as if they could hear with them and not with their ears. ... Some are always smiling and laughing at every word they speak, as if they were flirtatious girls or silly juggling jesters in search of attention.[11]

Standing between the contemplative and the transcendent god lies the cloud of unknowing, whose nature is, according to Spearing's translation, the bewitchment of imagistic or "sensory" language. The author monk evokes the most vivid imagery of sensuality, only to negate it in favour of the ineffable transcendent: "the imagination is stimulated to draw on the memories of daily experience stored in daily language [and then] ... the imagination is being forbidden to operate as it is compelled to operate."[12]

Along with the cloud of unknowing there is a cloud of forgetting which the contemplative must "set between himself and everything that is bodily and can be known". Getting beyond the cloud of unknowing is a matter for the will. Metaphors such as "piercing the darkness", "sharp dart", "beat," are used and thus "the world of the bodily senses is evoked in order to be dismissed, and yet evoked so vividly that we cannot in fact dismiss it."

It seems, then, that our epistemological tradition seeks crystal clarity and the certainty of the intoxicating heights, and in doing so, consigns ordinary life, the life of human beings, to the epistemological status of an amorphous fog. Jung's entire world of childhood was so demoted, and for Heidegger the entire empirical world became a fog beneath his feet.

There is one more famous historic reference to fogs in the western tradition. The well-known cliché, "the fog of war," arose in 1832, in a book, On War, by Carl von Clausewitz, a General in the Prussian army. Wikipedia offers this very pertinent citation of von Clausewitz's belief, "[h]e saw history as a vital check on erudite abstractions that did not accord with experience." He writes in his book on the fog of war:

> War is the realm of uncertainty; three quarters of the factors on which action in war is based are wrapped in a fog of greater or lesser uncertainty. A sensitive and discriminating judgment is called for; a skilled intelligence to scent out the truth.[13]

For von Clausewitz, the image of fog is the realm of uncertainty, associated with being "on the ground" in empirical reality and requiring a kind of animal sense to "scent out the truth." Whereas Heidegger privileged spacious mountain tops and clear skies with their infinite distances, von Clausewitz valued closeness, being on the ground, having to exercise judgment, no doubt on the spot, alert to changing circumstances and being able to adjust accordingly, and appropriately.

These rich amplifications arising from my research into our philosophical and epistemological tradition, and the human beings who could reach those heights, opened my eyes to the "fog" aspect of my dream and its meaning as it unfolded into the particulars of my life during the subsequent decades. I could now begin to see the fog, not just as an obstacle to seeing clearly, but as another way of seeing, of knowing the truth—a shift perhaps that my dream is suggesting as a factor in the little boy's healing.

End of the World

In the years that followed my dream, I entered the realm of living thinking ever more deeply, in the spirit that Arendt notes: "[w]e are so accustomed to the old oppositions of reason and passion, of mind and life, that the idea of passionate thinking, in which thinking and being alive become one, can be a bit startling."[14] I soared to the heights and encountered my version of the enormous transformations taking place in the psychic background of our times, i.e., "the [psychic—*my insert*] problem that is being played out in the world," as Jung says, or as Heidegger says, "the difficult becoming of a dark future." It seems that those human beings who are transported to those dizzying heights of the psychic background to empirical reality today will find some version or another of an "apocalypse" awaiting them, as the soul works its way through the end of (the logic of) one world and the birth of another.

The theme of end of the world was very much in vogue at the time of Heidegger and Jung, expressed as *fin de siècle* in Europe, around the end of the 19th century. This theme brought forward social theories of the degeneration of civilization and the need for a total rebirth. Another word that is used to express the same mood is "palingenesis", and this idea forms a central tenet of fascism:

> The mythic core in a single concept involved resuscitating what is an obscure and obsolescent word in English, 'palingenesis' (meaning rebirth), and coining the expression 'Palingenetic ultra-nationalism'. … generic fascism can be defined in terms of this expression… From this assumption about the matrix of fascist ideology, a number of features of generic fascism follow which have a profound bearing on how it operates in practice both as an opposition movement and as a regime.[15]

In Griffin's efforts to analyze the roots of fascism, he turns to Jung and then Campbell:

> It is worth adding that Campbell corroborates many of Jung's insights, particularly the distinction between a 'healthy mysticism' which 'goes beyond the whole field of separation', namely world-views which breed dualisms and divisions. The 'concretization of symbols' into historical facts and into political goals, to be realized at all costs, turns a cosmology promoting a healthy transcendence into one which breeds violence and hate: 'The Promised Land … has to do with what you're doing inside yourself, not whom you've got your weapons pointed at to kill. The shift is dramatic. And so you can say that history is simply a function of misunderstood mythology'.[16]

In quoting Campbell and through him, Jung, Griffin is reaching to find a "cause" of fascism, not in the empirical world where it plays out its horrors out to the detriment of all, but in the psychic/linguistic background of that empirical world—this background of course being Jung's primary psychological focus of concern throughout his life.

Individual human beings may indeed soar up to these heights of "passionate thinking", as Arendt says, and begin to think the movements of the living spirit which is beyond sensory intuition, beyond the imagination and its love of the sensual world. If they do so today, in modern times, they will find the turbulence of transformation as the psychic background constituting the contours of one world gives way to that of another. But to "get there", it appears that the entire world of the senses, the body and all empirical life must be negated, degraded to the logical status of a "fog."

This devaluing of ordinary empirical life is achieved by the will and its attendant moods of fascination, exhilaration, intoxication, and ecstasy, coupled with equal levels of dismissal, scorn, derogation and even contempt for what now lies amorphously beneath one's feet. All these aspects of the "mood of ascension" as we can call it, belong to the phenomenon of the apocalypse itself. They are all "of the spirit". To enter that domain of "passionate thinking" is to think it out in all its various aspects.

So what goes wrong? How does such a soaring exultant discovery of "pure spirit" working out its *telos*, and participating in that transformation, produce such devastating consequences across scale in the human realm of empirical reality, from individual human relationship to the destruction of nations? How does living thinking, or the sacred waters of life become the logic of fascism or totalitarianism?How does the logic of transformation become the logic of palingenesis? How does ecstatic experience become institutionalised and deadly?

These questions hinge on our forgetfulness, or not, of the *threshold*!

The Threshold & the Body

Owen Barfield gives us a clue, refining at the same time Campbell's simplistic aphorism that, "history is simply a function of misunderstood mythology."[17]

He begins with a discussion of the Bhagavad-Gita and the complex structure of consciousness that it represents: "two different planes of consciousness with what I will call a threshold between them." They are the planes of ordinary consciousness and visionary consciousness. He then proceeds to show how this ancient structure can help us to see the structure in our modern Western consciousness. His argument takes a full essay to elucidate so I will just paraphrase his conclusion: This ancient dual structure in consciousness is now to be found "within us," as the duality between imagination and inspiration but the phenomenology remains quite analogous to the ancient one. With this in mind we can proceed to his discussion of the threshold between the two planes of consciousness.

We need to heed the warnings from both the Gita and from William Blake, Barfield thinks. This is a warning to heed the threshold, not ignore it. The two sides need to be kept distinct from one another —distinct, not necessarily separate:

> Blake insisted on that "single vision" is disastrous. And here let me into interpose that imagination and a faculty of "double vision" seem indeed to be almost

inseparable. When Blake supposed someone asking him if, looking at the sun, he did not see "a round thing somewhat like a guinea," he replied: "Oh no, no, no, but an immeasurable company of the Heavenly Host crying Holy, Holy, Holy is the Lord and God Almighty." He did not in my view mean by this that he was incapable of also seeing something like a guinea. Had that been so, he would have been mad. Imagination, in fact, presupposes "double" vision and not simply the substitution of one kind of single vision for another. It requires a sober ability to have the thing both ways at once. May it not be that, if we have reached the stage at which both sides of the threshold allowed to be found "within" us, instead of one side being within and the other without—if what was once inspiration is now imagination—nevertheless we must not lose sight of the fact that there is still that threshold between them?[18]

If we do lose sight of the threshold and the need to keep both sides distinct, then Barfield tells us what happens next:

[w]e endeavour to speak, or even to think, of the further side in ideas formed only on this side, in categories of thought and modes of speech, which are almost by definition only applicable to this side. We therefore become exposed to a danger of seizing hold of and converting those "concrete inklings from beyond the threshold" into abstract propositions and getting more and more involved in a kind of spiders web of increasingly abstract, increasingly contentless, and increasingly sesquipedalion jargon, of which the final effect is only to fatigue and bewilder ourselves and our readers…[19]

Barfield then graphically describes a further danger most relevant to my discussion here:

> When the two opposite sides [of the threshold—*my insert*] are run together in the understanding, with the insulating membrane between them rudely torn and shattered, they explode in the resulting short circuit into a chaotic pus of the meaningless or the absurd.[20]

The insulating membrane, rudely torn and shattered, is a vivid and provocative image of what happens when aspects of the spiritual "phenomenon", call them figures of speech or originary language, are appropriated by the human spirit and wrenched back across the threshold, piercing empirical reality as literalisms, certainties, or as human abstract propositions: The poetry of "formation, transformation/ eternal Mind's eternal recreation" becomes the ideology of palingenesis—a self-justifying conceptual foundation for the establishment of the fascist State, or state of mind.

When the little boy in my dream has his first taste of thinking, he becomes trapped by what he saw. The image of a little boy trying to understand something of the psychic underpinnings of empirical reality points to my own immature attitude in relation to approaching such mysteries. He becomes fascinated by what he sees, anxiously striving to understand, without any of the preparations required for understanding. The "fixed" flies on the wall reflect his fixation with something that terrifies him. He tries to overcome his terror by mastering what is terrifying him. But he does not know what that terror is…

In 1985 and on for the next decade or so, I eagerly sought and was granted access across the threshold to visionary states of mind. It took me almost that long to realize that I was also terrified of those very heights. I eventually found my way to an Indian myth that could express my condition in a paradox: Terror-Joy![21] I lived that paradox. While I continued to push down the "cloud of forgetting" in my eager pursuit of "transcendent" spirit, my body increased its level of suffering. I developed symptoms of extreme heat so severe that my skin began to burn up. I kept going "up", thinking these symptoms were telling me that I was on the right path. And so they got worse.

Under the weight of the claims of the spirit, I still had to deal with the devastation of my outer life and my escalating impoverishment in the material realm. I finally entered my version of the dark night of the soul. I felt utterly abandoned by the community and equally abandoned by any spiritual advocate. My existential condition broke in one day while I was driving down the freeway. I suddenly realized how much I had lost. While others were living their lives with at least some degree of success, helping life continue in some way, I had, in contrast, lost years of achievement. My entire life was based on massive failures. At the same time I was led ineluctably to the threshold.

Living Thinking & The Threshold

When we cross the threshold, the "inklings" we receive, as Barfield says, are living figures of speech, or simply living thinking. They are self-referential, self-presencing, purely "fictional", and real! Nietzsche crossed the threshold and "lived to tell the tale." This rather extended passage vividly displays the phenomenology of his encounters:

> Has any one at the end of the nineteenth century any distinct notion of what poets of a stronger age

understood by the word inspiration? If not, I will describe it. If one had the smallest vestige of superstition in one, it would hardly be possible to set aside completely the idea that one is the mere incarnation, mouthpiece [my italics] or medium of an almighty power. The idea of revelation in the sense that something becomes suddenly visible and audible with indescribable certainty and accuracy, which profoundly convulses and upsets one—describes simply the matter of fact. One hears—one does not seek; one takes—one does not ask who gives: a thought suddenly flashes up like lightning, it comes with necessity, unhesitatingly—I have never had any choice in the matter. There is an ecstasy such that the immense strain of it is sometimes relaxed by a flood of tears, along with which one's steps either rush or involuntarily lag, alternately. There is the feeling that one is completely out of hand, with the very distinct consciousness of an endless number of fine thrills and quiverings to the very toes;—there is a depth of happiness in which the painfullest and gloomiest do not operate as antitheses, but as conditioned, as demanded in the sense of necessary shades of colour in such an overflow of light. There is an instinct for rhythmic relations which embraces wide areas of forms (length, the need of a wide-embracing rhythm, is almost the measure of the force of an inspiration, a sort of counterpart to its pressure and tension). Everything happens quite involuntarily, as if in a tempestuous outburst of freedom, of absoluteness, of power and divinity. The involuntariness of the figures and similes is the most remarkable thing; one loses all perception of what constitutes the figure and what constitutes the simile; everything seems to present itself as the readiest, the correctest and the simplest means of expression…[22]

Nietzsche physically suffered greatly throughout his life, but as we can see from the following short summary, no one, including Nietzsche it seems, can point to the cause of his illness *as residing in the manner Nietzsche crossed the threshold and returned*:

> Some argue that Nietzsche was afflicted with a syphilitic infection … some claim that his use of chloral hydrate, a drug which he had been using as a sedative, undermined his already-weakened nervous system; some speculate that Nietzsche's collapse was due to a brain disease he inherited from his father; some maintain that a mental illness gradually drove him insane; some maintain that he suffered from a slow-growing, frontal cranial base tumor; some maintain that he suffered from CADASIL syndrome, a hereditary stroke disorder. The exact cause of Nietzsche's incapacitation remains unclear.[23]

Like most modern individuals, Nietzsche's ordinary consciousness was in no way prepared for crossing the threshold. There is no evidence in Nietzsche's account that he even conceived of a threshold. He simply says, "… something becomes suddenly visible and audible with indescribable certainty and accuracy". In other words he is already on the other side, or on top of the mountain before he knows it. From his disclosive account of his visionary experiences, we can see how much he privileges the visionary experiences themselves over his mortality: "[t]here is the feeling that one is completely out of hand, with the very distinct consciousness of an endless number of fine thrills and quiverings to the very toes, etc.", "I never had any choice in the matter …"

Knowledge of the threshold is critical to a safe transition between planes of consciousness. Crossing the threshold, and returning, is fundamentally a matter of language—living embodied language. Human beings normally live on the ordinary plane of consciousness in which language is primarily understand as communication between people, a stable world constituted linguistically with abstract concepts and dead metaphors or tropes. When we cross the threshold, it is as Emerson says:

> The things we now esteem fixed shall, one by one, detach themselves, like ripe fruit, from our experience, and fall. The wind shall blow them none knows whither. The landscapes, the figures, Boston, London, are facts as fugitive as any institution past, or any whiff of mist or smoke, and so is society, and so is the world. The soul looketh steadily forwards, creating a world before her, leaving worlds behind her. She has no dates, nor rites, nor persons, nor specialties, nor men. The soul knows only the soul; the web of events is the flowing robe in which she is clothed.[24]

Fixed meanings blow away and we are confronted with fluid, conscious, living language with which we begin to participate, in its dynamism, not as "pure spirit" but as human spirit—and as such, our human body is included in some way that our culture has yet to bring to language on the ordinary plane of existence. We humans must "bodily" cross the threshold in some new sense of "body". Nietzsche speaks of "fine thrills and quiverings to the very toes," but he is experiencing this while in the ecstatic state i.e. from the other side of the threshold, so some real sense of "body" must have crossed with him, or as him. We can get a taste of this "embodied" state with this excerpt from one of my ecstasies:

> At the peak of my ecstasies, I meet the Beloved who comes to me while I am fully awake, alone in my bed. I can get out of bed and see quite clearly with my outer vision that I am alone yet I also see, feel, touch her

there beside me, as real as my knowledge that I was alone. Both realities are interpenetrating each other. Now I experience myself as being loved by another, an OTHER, totally— I am an object of divine desire. I learn through direct initiation through my own body that the human being is able to receive an influx of love from the Beyond. It is the organ of the heart that is the door and it is the belief systems of the ego that close the door. When I am afraid, in the closed bottle of my own ego, that I cannot contain it, I am told again and again by my divine lover that I can, that I need only to open up completely, right to the level of the cells of my body.[25]

The only way I can begin to articulate what is happening when the human spirit crosses the threshold "bodily" is to say that, in doing so, the body itself begins to come to language, to become conscious of itself as body, now living body, living language. An incarnation takes place in the realm of living embodied language, most often quite beyond the horizon of the reflective ego of the person. And then there is the return across the threshold into the plane of ordinary consciousness.

What goes wrong? How do the heights of ecstasy pervert into totalitarian ideology, or Nazism? Polt gives us a further clue when he poses a similar question regarding Heidegger's turn away from empathy and feeling in the 1930's. He seeks an answer within the texts of The Black Notebooks:

In the 1920's Heidegger scrutinized not just texts, but experience, and was able to show that the usual metaphysical concepts were inadequate to that experience. He was able to build new subtle concepts that were flexible enough to point to the wealth of human life. Now [i.e. in the 1930's—*my insert*] Heidegger sees that human life is itself is determined by metaphysics. The only alternative is a new inception.[26]

Polt demonstrates that a reversal took place in Heidegger. In the 1920's he crossed the threshold and found a new kind of more flexible, fluid thinking, and he returned his "spiritual treasures" in service of humankind. In the 1930's a complete reversal took place, where humankind became subordinate to his *palingenetic* thinking.[27] It was that thinking that now mattered to Heidegger, not people. The thinking that properly belongs on the other side of the threshold was usurped and appropriated to Heidegger's human ends, and so perverted.

Polt goes on to note that Heidegger records a moment where he could hear his innermost voice and chose to steel himself against it, in favour of plunging ever more deeply into the "difficult becoming of a dark future." This move seems to a potent example of how a genuine soul movement in the plane of inspiration becomes "fixed" and translated into a "prophecy" or prediction on the plane of ordinary reality, at the expense of his humanness. A soul truth becomes a literal "truth" for empirical reality, with all the devastating consequences that seared the heart of the world in the 20th century.

This peril can be further amplified by a description of the nature of "true" thinking, i.e. "in contrast to the perception of the sensory world and to the mythic image or the imaginable," offered by Wolfgang Giegerich:

> True thought, because it is not concerned with what we think, is restless, merciless (which is an effect of it's cold, underworldly nature). Professional. What we feel and whether we welcome what it reveals and where it leads is of no significance. It is concerned with truth. Thinking is not for sissies. One must not show too

much of a soft spot for our personal feelings nor for the images in their innocent beauty nor for the things of the world in their natural appearance, nor cleaning too much to our desire for unbroken continuity, all of which points to a defence against the underworldly soul, to a wish to hold on to the day world.[28]

This description of the true nature of thinking, the kind of thinking that Heidegger and Nietzsche discovered on crossing the threshold, hints strongly at what can and indeed happens to the unprepared human being who crosses the threshold and participates in such an "alien phenomenon" (i.e. begins to think that thinking as it thinks itself out in his or her mind). If the visionary side of the threshold is, in one way or another, privileged by the "thinker", then those non-human qualities of "true thinking" incarnate "within" the ordinary consciousness of the human being, upon his or her return. The non-human qualities become in effect inhuman attitudes towards our fellows, with, at times, devastating consequences to the lives of human beings, across scale.

The Threshold & Art

Artists seem generally more aware of the existence of the threshold, its gifts, and its dangers. In contrast to those who seek only to "transcend" and abide in the heights of "pure thinking", many artists point to the central importance of the threshold, and the necessity of holding its presence in full consciousness while traversing the plane of visionary consciousness. They call the threshold by various names—trance state, hypnagogic states, or as I do, simply the "in between" state. For example, Hirsch cites the efforts of Edgar Allen Poe:

who gave a powerfully clinical analysis of a passive state that he was learning to control: " now, so entire is my faith in the power of words, that, at times, I have believed it possible to embody even the evanescence of fancies such as I have attempted to describe. In experiments with this end in view, I have proceeded so far as, first, to control… the existence of the condition …" Poe suggests that he was learning to prevent his daydreaming state from lapsing into sleep, to startle it into wakefulness and then transfer it into the realm of memory to continue the condition… where he could write it into being, invoking and enacting its presence in language.[29]

Hirsch goes on to warn, "[i]t is too reductive to think of artistic creation as merely putting oneself in a trance state. We need a fresh vocabulary, a fuller and more enhanced notion of the artistic trance state in which one also actively thinks."

Indeed we do! The stakes couldn't be higher. Knowledge of the threshold and its phenomenology is critical to the issue of staying human, while crossing and returning from the threshold. We do seem to have unparalleled access to the realm of living thinking today. We simplistically call it "creativity", shamanic ecstasies, inspiration, and so on. This plane of extraordinary consciousness is eagerly sought, the poet seeking a domain where he can

wed common language to an indescribable atmosphere, where he can identify a 'poetic constant' and unify it with themes of the moment, 'themes so overbearing that they must be expressed at any cost'.[30]

The artist enters a state of "lucid delirium," or "inspiration and control over the inspiration."[31] Yet we mostly approach the visionary plane of consciousness with self-serving interests, not having a clue about what crosses over the threshold with us through and within language, once we return. Our ordinary human discourse now carries a "alien" within its syntax—a non-human element that works its will through us in the form of "institutional" or ideological thinking, subsuming human warmth and community under its now abstract propositions.

In my dream, the little boy is transfixed by a vision that he does not understand, and he makes a drawing that he shows the doctor. When I woke up from the dream, I drew my version of the scene of little flies fixed behind a fly swatter. This artistic response is another way to cross the threshold and return—a way that is close to Barfield's suggestion, asking what kind of language will preserve the threshold, the distinction between the two sides, and allow "effective and badly needed inspirations from beyond the threshold ... [to be] either uttered or apprehended." If this language is achieved, then

> the threshold becomes like Aladdin's ring, yielding new meanings for old and giving birth to a future that has originated in present creativity instead of being a helpless copy of the outwardly observed forms of the past."[32]

What happened as I drew a picture of the dream, i.e., of the drawing the little boy made? I did not attempt to accurately reproduce the boy's drawing, based on ordinary consciousness' interpretation of "flies" and "swatters". To do that is to literalise fluid meaning, to fix it in the categories of experience that properly belong only to this side of the threshold, in this case our ordinary understanding of flies and fly swatters. This is how soul truths are perverted into ideologies, or as

Barfield puts it, how the insulating membrane between the two planes of consciousness is rudely torn and shattered. Soul truths draw from empirical reality in order to speak but their "speech" does not refer simply to that empirical reality. Even mythical beasts such as Pegasus draw from natural wings and horses, in order for that unnatural figure to "speak" its soul truth to us. The little boy drawing a picture of flies killed and fixed by fly swatters is not referring to a natural event, but to a soul matter which I had not yet learned to think.

When I woke up from the dream, my psyche was already in movement, stimulated by the dream, in two different directions at once. At first I quickly drew a sketch in response to the little boy's drawing and immediately noticed that this image was moving from flies, to rocket ships, to Cartesian grids, to phalli, to fly swatters. Instead of allowing that movement to continue with further drawings, further artistic expression, I became filled with the same urgency that the little boy had, to think the meaning of the grid, revealing my secret identification with that dream figure. In the face of great uncertainty, even the terror of not knowing, as I said above, I headed for the exhilarating heights of certainty and so my path was laid down for many years.

Although I downplayed my initial artistic impulse following my dream, I did not condemn it to the Cloud of Forgetting. The fact that I wrote my dream down in the first place, and responded to it with real action in the world, was a seed of a future development, best characterized as love and devotion to the dream. After all, the dream's effect impelled me more deeply into life's complexities, even as I tried to conquer those complexities with the certainty of understanding. For many years I oscillated between two poles, that of the "thinker", and "artist", and these oscillations have played throughout my essays and books. I think they are evident even in this essay.

I have been working for many years now to try to say this configuration of extraordinary consciousness co-present with ordinary consciousness, to bring its speech into actuality through some kind of art form. My 1985 dream in effect initiated me into this task by producing what appeared at the time to be two contradictory movements in me after the dream: striving for the heights of clear thinking beyond empirical reality, and remaining on the ground with all its uncertainties and complexities. The tension between the movements almost tore me in two, at times. But I kept writing, no matter what.

A New Genre?

Is it possible to write in a way that is both participatory and reflective? We simply do not have the language to describe such a form of consciousness. This is because our language is rooted in the plane of ordinary consciousness only, i.e. our language and cultural forms are expressions of reflection, not participation in the *other*.

In my efforts to find such a genre, I earlier attempted to characterise this form of writing as:

> A spontaneous weaving of realities that we normally keep well apart. This writing moves from a memory to a dream to a reflection of an external event, to an etymological study of a word, to the words of another author until the usual separation of inner and outer dissolves…

There is not so much an oscillation between ordinary reflections (memory) and inspiration, or rather, it can begin that way, but the tempo increases and a fluid state of mind/body ensues. I may, for example be quite lucidly researching a memory or text, when another memory or even a kind of *poesis* ("delirium") emerges through my reflections. The crucial ego element in this unsettling experience is to give way to the strange new visitor and allow it to speak. When it has "spoken", further deliberations can occur, until the next exchange occurs. Sometimes this movement is furious and, because I am poor typist, I have to revert quickly to technical devices such as voice-to-script in order to keep up with the torrent. Some of my books have been written this way, in four or five days of intense "passionate thinking".

If we consider this kind of writing to be related to the critical question of the threshold and the two planes of consciousness, then two languages should be distinguishable, while simultaneously, some sense of an "in between" comes into presence as the two languages interpenetrate. I must leave my reader to make his or her own judgments regarding my "success", but I think my description of the desired qualities of this "new genre" does approach the domain of interest that Barfield and Hirsch are exploring too.

It seems that Heidegger was on this trail too. He wrote one book that stands apart from all his others in its style and intention: Written in 1936-38, Contributions to Philosophy draws this observation from Richard Polt:

> There is less consensus about this book then about nearly any other 20th century philosophical text. Is it "Heidegger's major at work" or "metaphysical

dadaism"? An earthshaking achievement or laughable gibberish? … why is it so turbulent and esoteric?[33]

Polt's book is a sustained effort to address his claim that Heidegger's "Contributions are repeated attempts to participate in an event of appropriation, that is more fundamental than any theoretical truth."[34]

To understand this tightly packed statement a little better, we can turn to Polt's interpretations of Heidegger's attitude towards poetry:

> The goal of poetry is to rejuvenate and transform our ways of perceiving what is—in other words, to participate in and even "found" the emergence of meaning, the event of be-ing. How does this differ from bethinking? Does poetry experience the world as if for the first time, while philosophy experiences it as if for the last? For the poet, things are wondrous—even an old man or a familiar ruin are encountered with an arresting strangeness, so that we see them as they have never been seen before. Poetry opens new prospects. But philosophy typically takes a retrospective position, summing up the sense of all that has unfolded… But these thoughts will not apply perfectly to Heidegger.[35]

In Contributions, Heidegger is exploring the closeness to poetry of a new kind of futural philosophy. The initially troubling word, "appropriation" with its connotations of wilfulness, does evoke a notion of seizing, but also of being seized, being owned and owning, all in the sense of bringing new meaning into being, for the first time. I think Heidegger is here exploring the phenomenon of the threshold—what he calls "being-there" but he seems to lack a poetic touch, "[t]he style borrows from Nietzsche's Zarathustra and Hölderlin's hymns, without attaining the grace of either writer."[36]

As I read the portions of Contributions that concern people, I discovered a cold distance from the lives of ordinary human beings, including Heidegger's humanness, reminding me that he wrote this book in the pivotal 1930's when he turned away from the warmth of human relationship, to the heights of spirit. In §248, he speaks of the "future ones." He speaks of people, for example in a completely abstract and removed manner, valorising distance as "the greatest":

> A people is a people only if it receives its history as allotted to it through finding its god, the god that compels this people beyond itself and this places the people back amid beings... Hölderlin approaches the future ones from the farthest away and accordingly is their most futural poet. Hölderlin is the most futural because he approaches from the longest distance and in this distance traverses and transforms what is greatest."[37]

If Contributions is his attempt to investigate the threshold between two planes of consciousness, then it is a clear failure because the language of the ordinary plane is totally absent. We do not hear from the man Heidegger at all, for example. He is talking from the mountaintop, making pronouncements to the fog below.

If we are to participate with extraordinary consciousness, we must do so with our full humanness, holding the two sides in a creative tension across the threshold, so that new language may be born that is true to the reality of what Barfield calls "noetic vision," as in my dream-visions. Barfield offers us some conditions that have to be met for this kind of new language:

> [T]he poets, from Dante to the Romantics, have been experimenting [with this problem of language—my

insert]; and the question arises for me whether it can any longer be safely left in their hands alone, especially as there is an increasing tendency on their part to disclaim all responsibility for it… I am persuaded that the problem cannot even be fruitfully debated except on the basis of the three positions I have been seeking to establish: (1) that there is such a thing as noetic vision… ; (2) that this is a philosophical as well as an aesthetic problem; (3) that the act of vision, though not the objective content of the vision, requires the maintenance, and not the sacrifice, of ordinary consciousness.[38]

To Conclude: A Dream

This essay seems to be drawing to a close as I can feel a "withdrawal" taking place. Whatever was present guiding my hand and supporting this work is done, for now. It may be that an aspect of my inevitable entanglement in the logic of my 1985 dream has completed itself and withdrew, in the writing of this essay. At the time of beginning this essay I had the following dream:

> I am with a panel of three men. They say I can study German. They have selected me. One takes me to jewellery shop and says I may select a gold watch. I choose one.

The dream pairs a new possibility ("can") or commencement, with retirement (the gold watch). For many years I have been learning to think the thought of Continental philosophy. My eager pursuit of the power of this thinking left me blinded to the threshold and I did not notice that, as much as I was thinking that thought, it was thinking me. I leaped to the mountaintop and felt the exhilaration of seeing vast distances clearly.

The vista of history opened up to me. I eagerly assimilated Heidegger's view of the history of being with its five or six epochs, each separated by the inception of an entirely new world of appearances. I loved Giegerich's psychological view of history as a series of involutions in which the soul further reflects on itself—each age therefore sublating all former ages as moments within its logic. I worked hard to understand Barfield's view of history as a history of the evolving polar relationship between consciousness and world.

The vista of space also opened up for me and I began to absorb the language of worldviews. Heidegger taught me how the very notion of a worldview is a thoroughly modern one, through which we view our past, for example. Giegerich showed me how the language of worldviews belongs to the logic of our technological civilization, and how everything empirical—you, me, natural animals, things—is now sublated as moments within an overarching language of abstraction, totality, "world."

O yes, this was heady, intoxicating. I could now see so much and was quite blinded to where I had to be in order to see this way. I was in outer space, or on the highest mountain, way above the Cloud of Unknowing, and at the very same time, unbeknownst to me, something from those airy heights had incarnated in me, through language, and was beginning to work its way into the world, while I danced in the mountain air.

My wife began to notice that, at times, I held a somewhat disdainful attitude towards others in ordinary conversation at home. Sometimes this disdain moved closer to dismissal or contempt. My response was always in terms of optical metaphors, "they just don't see!"

Apparently there was only one way to see—my way! My scorn grew proportionally to my certainty. When I did speak in groups, sometimes my speech would start to sound like a rant—and right now I have an image of Hitler speaking (yelling) at Nuremberg, intruding in on my writing. Yes, that's it! I was becoming totalitarian in my attitude towards other human beings.

Well, there is nothing like getting a dose of what you dish out to others, in order to effect a cure! I managed to join an organization that dished it out measure for measure. Over a period of years my writings were dismissed, disparaged, mocked and "corrected". I gave as good as I got. Whenever I wrote a piece that was critical, or even different from what was fast becoming a "received canon of thought," I found, in the act of writing, that I became very careful about putting things precisely this way and not that, even down to punctuation, vocabulary, sentence construction. I was developing paranoid fantasies, already anticipating attacks, even before I posted the article, wrote the essay etc. Although my "paranoia" always proved to be a real fear (I was in fact attacked mercilessly), I could not account for the paranoid fantasies, or the virulence of the attacks, or indeed the violence of my reactions.

After considerable suffering, and occasional exultations of victory, but no joy, I finally turned to the task of studying the phenomenon, rather than reacting to it, or starting battles that left me utterly frustrated. I began to read other authors who were addressing similar issues, in relation to this organization. I also focused on the mood of the literature associated with this organization. This mood can be characterized as one of "eliminating the opposition," by a kind of literary carpet-bombing, intent on leaving no man standing. There was no room for alternate voices, or perspectives, or any uncertainty. What increasingly mattered was an emerging canon of thought, one way of thinking about things, one way of formulating issues—a totalitarian "state of mind" was being born, in language.

My insight into the totalitarian mood saturating the literature of this organization occurred as this new dream came through. The dream shows the difference between what I had up to this time been doing (learning to think in a totalitarian way) and studying the phenomenon of totalitarianism. In learning how to study the phenomenon, the dream suggests I am also retiring (from battle?).

This essay is the fruit of my study and in writing it I am free of that incursion, into the ordinary plane of consciousness, of what properly belongs on the other side of the threshold. I had ignored the threshold in my attraction to the heights of a worldview, and paid the price.

I was wrenched away from an unconscious identification with the language of "[t]rue thought, … not concerned with what we think, … restless, merciless (which is an effect of it's cold, under-worldly nature)" by the one power that can compete with such a phenomenon—human love and community. I was given feedback from someone I love and she matters to me, even though for some time I resisted, on the self-justifying basis of feeling misunderstood. So we argued, but I did not consign her to the Cloud of Forgetting. She did not become an abstraction (one of Heidegger's "the people"), although on occasion I did say, in effect, that she is "just like the others". Can you hear the dismissive contempt and consignment to abstraction in that terrible charge?

From 1985 to 2015, full circle—a completion of sorts! Perhaps one more thing, on a dark note! In 1994, while I was living in Seattle, I gave a talk at the C. G. Jung Society there. The title of it was Psychopathy in Everyday Life. Already I had some glimmerings of what was to become clearer, in 2015. I tried to show that the psychopath is not only a particular, virulent kind of personality that we all should be wary of, but that psychopathic gestures are working every day, through each us, at the level of language. I gave many examples from the workplace. For example, an employee may be causing trouble and management responds with, "let's just get rid of him!"

Once you catch on to the language structure, you can start to perceive its magnitude, working quietly within, and as, our everyday language—the incarnation of a totalitarian "state of mind", no longer needing literal political institutions to enact its mission of palingenesis, working quietly to eliminate anything human, anything to do with love, anything to do with community.

---

[1] For the full story, see: Woodcock, J. C. The Imperative. CreateSpace, 2015.

[2] Giegerich, W. "The Rocket and the Launching Base or The Leap from the Imaginal into Outer Space Named Reality" in Technology and the Soul (New Orleans, Spring Journal Books, 2007).

[3] Giegerich explore the historical roots of the fixed perspective, or staring in his latest book The Historical Emergence of the I

[4] Polt, R. The Emergency of Being: On Heidegger's Contributions to Philosophy (London. Cornell University Press, 2006).

5 Polt, R. "Heidegger's Black Notebook: Politics, Philosophy, Anti-Semitism", at Emory University, Sep. 5-6, 2014.

6 My transcription

7 Ibid

8 Ibid. Also see my book cover on page 1 above.

9 Jung, C. G. (Ed) Jaffé, A.: Memories, Dreams, Reflections (New York, Vintage. 1989), 32-3.

10 Ibid, 180.

11 Spearing, A. C. (tr.). The Cloud of Unknowing (London. Penguin, 2001).

12 Ibid, xxvii, xxx, xxxv

13 von Clausewitz, C.: vom Kriege 1873

14 From Arendt's radio address of 1969: "Martin Heidegger is Eighty Years Old".

15 Griffin, R. (ed.). *Fascism*. Oxford Readers Paperback, 1995, 4.

16 Griffin, R. *The Nature of Fascism*. NY. Routledge, 1993, 189.

17 Barfield, O. "Imagination and Inspiration" in The Rediscovery of Meaning. San Rafael. The Barfield Press, 1977, 128.

18 Ibid.

19 Ibid.

20 Ibid.

21 Taken from Joseph Campbell's story, "The Four Treasure-Seekers" from the Panchatantra in Myths to Live By (New York. Penguin, 1972), 222.

22 Nietzsche, F. Common, T. (tr.): "Introduction" in Thus Spake Zarathustra.

23 Wicks, R.: "Friedrich Nietzsche" in Stanford Encyclopedia of Philosophy, http://plato.stanford.edu/entries/nietzsche

[24] Emerson R.W.: The Oversoul. Found at: https://emersoncentral.com/texts/essays-first-series/the-over-soul/.

[25] See my Poems of Making, Poems of Death

[26] Polt, R.: "Heidegger's Black Notebook: Politics, Philosophy, Anti-Semitism", at Emory University, Sep. 5-6, 2014.

[27] Palingenesis as the core Revolutionary sentiment: "that privileged moment when frustration and despair in the contemporary state of human affairs are suddenly transfigured into the visionary sense of an imminent metamorphosis, a new world." From the Preface of: Griffin, R. The Nature of Fascism, 1993.

[28] Giegerich, W. The Soul Always Thinks. New Orleans. Spring Journal Books, 2010, 18.

[29] Hirsch, E. The Demon and the Angel (Orlando. Harcourt, 2002,) 102-3.

[30] Ibid, 101 *ff.*

[31] Ibid, 104.

[32] Barfield, O.: The Rediscovery of Meaning, 145, 147.

[33] Polt, R. The Emergency of Being: On Heidegger's Contributions to Philosophy. London. Cornell University Press, 2006, 1, 10.

[34] Polt, Richard. The Emergency of Being . Cornell University Press. Kindle Edition. Loc. 2367.

[35] Ibid, 114.

[36] Ibid, 2.

[37] Heidegger, M. Sallis, J. (ed.), Rojcewicz, R. & Vallega-Neu, D. (tr.).: Contributions to Philosophy. (Bloomington. Indian University Press, 2012).

[38] Barfield, O. The Rediscovery of Meaning, 1977, 34.

SOUL IN OBLIVION

C. G. Jung discovered and committed his life's work to the reality of the objective psyche or soul. Since his death in 1961, the move away from soul as a reality has become the hallmark of philosophy, psychology, and many other disciplines. When technology was invented to scan the human brain, this move accelerated dramatically and this essay explores the almost universal denial of the reality of soul in the "official narratives" of our Western culture. The ever-astute educator, George Orwell, in his famous little book, 1984, exposes the intimate connection between language and soul (or its demise) this way:

> "It's a beautiful thing, the destruction of words. Of course the great wastage is in the verbs and adjectives, but there are hundreds of nouns that can be got rid of as well …You haven't a real appreciation of Newspeak, Winston," he said almost sadly… "Don't you see that the whole aim of Newspeak is to narrow the range of thought? In the end we shall make thought crime literally impossible, because there will be no words in which to express it. Every concept that can ever be needed, will be expressed by exactly one word, with its meaning rigidly defined and all its subsidiary meanings rubbed out and forgotten."

Any writer like me who bases his entire body of work on the reality of soul would be wise to comprehend and come to terms with the prevailing attitude of complete denial of soul (often dismissed as the god of the gaps i.e. an unnecessary obfuscating concept used when we have a temporary lack of empirical knowledge).

In 2007, TIME magazine published a special edition on the brain: The Mystery of Consciousness.[1] Various recognized experts in the fields of brain research and consciousness were interviewed and so the articles explored the latest findings, theories, and difficulties surrounding the "mind-body" problem, or how consciousness and the brain are related.

Much of the discussion focuses on the scientific breakthroughs made possible by MRI scans of the brain. Further discussions use the amassing body of evidence from these increasingly sensitive and precise measurements in order to develop theories of consciousness, or mind, or us as *seemingly* self-aware beings.

These articles, though not comprehensive or exhaustive, and intended for a general audience, do show the emergence of a growing consensus amongst foremost researchers concerning the nature and provenance of consciousness and therefore us, as mental beings. We are in the process of forming a new set of collective representations about us and our bodies, and this set is taking hold of our imaginations fast (if I may use that word any more–and there is doubt that I will be able to). We are quickly becoming accustomed or habituated to seeing ourselves a certain way and we may soon *become* that certain way.[2]

MRI scans, along with more invasive investigations, show conclusively how much consciousness and the brain are tied together, to use a loose term for a moment. As Steven Pinker says, "… consciousness can be pushed around by physical manipulations."

He cites electrical stimulation, chemicals, and radical surgeries, as examples of interventions that manipulate consciousness. Physical death means as far as anyone can know, death of consciousness. Even out-of-body experiences can be manipulated by stimulating the appropriate areas of the brain. Every activity of consciousness is rapidly being associated with a physical area of the brain, to the extent that Pinker can claim that, "cognitive scientists can almost read people's thoughts from the blood flow in their brains." [3]

From these incontestable facts a dominant theory has emerged: consciousness is an emergent property of biology! All experts cited by Pinker in his article share this theory universally.

Colin McGinn: "Nevertheless, consciousness is surely a natural biological product as devoid of the otherworldly as digestion ..."

Michael Gazzaniga: "Consciousness is an emergent property and not a process in and of itself. Our cognitive capacities reflect distributed processes throughout the brain."

Bernard Baars: "The topic of consciousness is much like sex in the Victorian age. Scientifically sex is just another part of biology ..."

Antonio Damasio: "All the natural history required to understand consciousness is now readily available in evolutionary biology and psychology."

Daniel Dennett, as paraphrased by Pinker: "Anything you would do to understand consciousness—like finding out what wavelengths make people see green ... boils down to information processing in the brain ..." [4]

This theory of mental processes emerging from physical ones has of course been around before brain research really accelerated with MRI technology but now it seems universally accepted amongst experts, almost a habit of thought, a common sense starting point to all further examination of consciousness and its relation to the brain.

Thus, we are collectively thinking of ourselves (our consciousness thinking about itself and its origins) as biological products, our provenance lies exclusively in the physical or biological domains. Therefore, the processes of biology are the processes of consciousness. For example, when biological processes come to an end so does consciousness. If biological processes are determined by evolutionary principles (such as survival, adaptation, competition etc.) then so is consciousness.

This way of thinking about others and ourselves is thus becoming a collective representation and for many people it is already so.

Although Pinker gives greatest weight to these researchers of the brain and its processes, he does give a nod to an understandable hesitation on the part of many "nonscientists" to think of themselves that way. But Pinker's nod is only for the sake of an easy dismissal of such complaints. He says for example that some people (apparently not worth naming alongside the experts that he is aligned with) see the Hard Problem of consciousness as an opportunity to "sneak the soul back in." Note the pejorative term "sneak." These anonymous people are sneaky. He dismisses such attempts as nothing more than a renaming of the Hard Problem: the mystery of consciousness becomes the mystery of the soul and we are none the wiser.

In this kind of easy dismissal Pinker joins the official narrative which eschews any version of a God of the Gaps i.e. any attempt to fill our present gaps in knowledge with an unnecessary obfuscating term like god, or soul or similar untestable idea. Instead he shows his allegiance to an unassailable optimism of modern researchers. As Colin McGinn puts it, "why is it (consciousness) so hard to tame scientifically? The answer, I suggest, lies not in the stars (god of the gaps), but in ourselves; our brains have not evolved with the necessary equipment to resolve this mystery."[5]

We can hear the resounding optimistic "yet" coursing through his argument. We don't need god because we only have to wait until our brains or our knowledge can fill in those temporary gaps.

In a small token of recognition Pinker mentions one (and only one) author who holds arguments counter to the prevailing one that he, Pinker, and a host of others hold dearly. But he does so only to dismiss it again, almost casually as if the counter argument does not even really warrant such a waste of ink. The author is Tom Wolfe who wrote an essay: Sorry, but Your Soul Just Died.

Wolfe's essay may be seen as succinct summary and critique of the new neurosciences and their theoretical forays into the theory of consciousness. He begins with:

> Brain imaging was invented for medical diagnosis. But its far greater importance is that it may very well confirm, in ways too precise to be disputed, certain theories about "the mind," "the self," "the soul and "free will" that are already devoutly believed in by scholars in what is now the hottest field in the academic world, neuroscience. [6]

He goes on to identify the central issue that neuroscience is concerned with today:

> We now live in an age in which science is a court from which there is no appeal. And the issue this time around, at the end of the twentieth century, is not the evolution of the species, which can seem a remote business, but the nature of our own precious inner selves.[7]

He addresses the same theory of consciousness that

Pinker espouses in his article: the theory that asserts consciousness is a product of brain processes. He examines the rippling effect of this theory out from the specialty of neuroscience into the wider worlds of politics, psychiatry, education, sociology, and so on. He gives many examples of the consequences when we begin to regard one another as pre-determined biological entities in all respects. That is to say, Wolfe provides us with an early glimpse of what lies in store for us if the dominant theory of consciousness provided by neuroscience becomes a collective representation:

> Eventually, as brain imaging is refined, the picture may become as clear and complete as those see-through exhibitions, at auto shows, of the inner workings of the internal combustion engine. At that point it may become obvious to everyone that all we are looking at is a piece of machinery, an analogy chemical computer, that processes information from the environment. "All," since you can look and look and you will not find any ghostly self inside, or any mind, or any soul.
>
> Thereupon, in the year 2006 or 2026, some new Nietzsche will step forward to announce: "The self is dead"—except that being prone to the poetic, like Nietzsche, he will probably say: "The soul is dead." He will say that he is merely bringing the news, the news of the greatest event of the millennium: "The soul, that last refuge of values, is dead, because educated people no longer believe it exists." Unless the assurances of the Wilsons and the Dennetts and the Dawkinses also start rippling out, the lurid carnival that will ensue may make the phrase "the total eclipse of all values" seem tame.[8]

Wolfe ends with an apocalyptic vision of science finally turning on itself with its own skepticism:

> I suddenly had a picture of the entire astonishing edifice

collapsing and modern man plunging headlong back into the primordial ooze. He's floundering, sloshing about, gulping for air, frantically treading ooze, when he feels something huge and smooth swim beneath him and boost him up, like some almighty dolphin. He can't see it, but he's much impressed. He names it God.

That may be but Pinker acknowledges none of Wolfe's examples and counter arguments. He off-handedly dismisses the entire essay with the comment that Wolfe has it backwards, that biology offers a far sounder basis for morality than Wolfe's "unproven dogma of an immortal soul". Far from agreeing with Wolfe's prognosis of a future in which the phrase "the total collapse of values" will seem tame, Pinker offers what seems to me a naïve argument in an attempt to gain further support for his own dogma of biology first – consciousness second. In so doing he inadvertently invokes a word that has long belonged to the domain of the soul: He says:

> Yet once we realize that our own consciousness is a product of our brains and that other people have brains like ours, a denial of other people's sentience becomes ludicrous … The undeniable fact that we are all made of the same flesh makes it impossible to deny our common capacity to *suffer* (my emphasis).[9]

Wolfe went to considerable trouble in his essay, the same one that Pinker dismisses, to demonstrate that, in *fact* (a term Pinker loves) people are not behaving the way Pinker wishes they would, when they learn about their biological pre-determinism. On the contrary they are coming up with ways to dehumanize one another with alarming frequency:

> The male of the human species is genetically hardwired to be polygamous, i.e., unfaithful to his legal mate. Any

magazine–reading male gets the picture soon enough. (Three million years of evolution made me do it!) Women lust after male celebrities, because they are genetically hardwired to sense that alpha males will take better care of their offspring. (I'm just a lifeguard in the gene pool, honey.) Teenage girls are genetically hardwired to be promiscuous and are as helpless to stop themselves as dogs in the park. (The school provides the condoms.) Most murders are the result of genetically hardwired compulsions. (Convicts can read, too, and they report to the prison psychiatrist: "Something came over me ... and then the knife went in".)[10]

Somehow Pinker's sunny theory of the genesis of morality sinks into the morass when confronted with such undeniable facts!

Pinker is quick to identify and eschew Wolfe's "dogma" of an immortal soul but it does seem easy to identify the other fellow's dogma while remaining blind to one's own. The theory of consciousness that states that consciousness emerges from matter persists in the face of a difficulty that is recognized by neuroscience as a formidable one. How DO physical processes lead to mental ones? Neuroscience has no answer but blithely proceeds anyway on the optimistic basis that, if not now, we soon will know (no god of the gaps, remember). So this difficulty, far from being seen as an insurmountable obstacle to the theory, is simply set aside as more evidence amasses showing an indubitable connection between mental and physical states. In other words, when a possible contraindication to the theory arises, it is simply put aside and the theory proceeds unmodified in any way. As Colin McGinn says:

> The paradox of the mind-body problem is that the explanatory causes of consciousness in the brain are not

discoverable by inspecting the brain, and introspection cannot reveal the rootedness of consciousness in brain tissue…. Nevertheless, consciousness is surely a natural biological product …[11]

Right from the outset, conceptual difficulties are announced and then dismissed. Only those findings that support the theory are let in. Nothing can challenge such a "theory" which appears more and more like, well, a dogma: a belief system that is improvable. Once such a habit of thought is entrenched it tends to assimilate new facts to itself and excludes any facts that challenge it. I think we can observe this process in the current "theory" of consciousness.

If a dogmatic point of view is holding people in thrall we may gain some insight into the phenomenon by studying its history. There is famous example of the early 20th century which illustrates this habit of thought and its power to enthrall: Freud's theory of seduction. He made a pioneering step of examining (unconscious) mental states in order to find causes for otherwise inexplicable physical states (such as hysterical blindness etc.)

Freud could not accept what his own clinical expertise was telling him. Mental states are "causing" physical ones, i.e. the mental state is prior, and the physical is secondary. Instead, his theory of neurosis and his developmental theory posit a physical cause prior to the observed mental state, which admittedly is still prior to the physical symptom in the adult. At first he proposed concrete sexual assault on the child as the physical cause. This step alienated him professionally for many years so he tried another form of the seduction theory which spoke of sexual fantasy (his version of the oedipal myth for example) that lies darkly in the child's unconscious mind.

This theory seems at first to be friendlier to the view that mental states can be ontologically prior to physical ones until we read his account of how these childhood fantasies come about:

> In inquiring into the origin of incest dread it could be expected that here also is the choice between possible explanations of a sociological, biological, and psychological nature in which the psychological motives might have to be considered as representative of biological forces.

He then appeals to Darwin's explanation which he calls a historic explanation. Drawing from current studies of apes and believing Darwin's account of the origin of mankind, Freud concocts a story of the genesis of the incest taboo:

> Let us now envisage the scene of such a totem meal and let us embellish it further with a few probable features that could not be adequately considered before … One day the expelled brothers … slew and ate the father … Of course these cannibal savages ate their victim … the totem feast, which is perhaps mankind's first celebration, would be the repetition and commemoration of this memorable criminal act, with which so many things began, social organization, moral restrictions and religion. [12]

When Freud could no longer locate the cause of adult neurosis in physical childhood trauma he reached into the deep past, armed with Darwin's vision of our evolution, and "found" a physical trauma which could cause the mental state of the neurotic (presence of forbidden desires etc.)

Like modern neuroscience, Freud proposed his theory and made the facts fit, ignoring other equally plausible theories such as the one that could have accounted easily for his clinical findings: mental states are prior to physical ones. Again like modern neuroscience, theoretical distortions are introduced and then eschewed so that the dogma may succeed. For example, how can a physical trauma putatively occurring millennia ago affect the mental state of a modern person? Freud's answer is through the mechanism of inherited memory. But how well can a concept of inherited memory (a mental state) fit with a purely biological account of our origins?

We can go even further back than Freud, before Darwin, and discover that a movement towards the dogma of "physical first, then mental" was emerging in the use of language, following Descartes' famous division between material objects of the world and the immaterial subject (consciousness). This division immediately caused problems since animals and plants were placed on the side of matter, yet were clearly different from rocks and minerals. A further division therefore emerged between animate matter and inanimate matter in the late 18th century.

Prior to the Cartesian division, matter was experienced as an indivisible whole called life, or even existence. Material existence had a mental and physical aspect. Our ancestors did not think about those aspects in the way of opposites, as we do today. So the later division into animate and inanimate matter, or as we would say today, living tissue and corpse is a very uncomfortable one that has led to the predicament of neuroscience, which is forced to ask the contorted question: how does a mental state arise from living tissue, when hidden, unexamined in the question is the answer: living tissue! The concept of *living* tissue can only mean a reference to a totality of mental and physical states, or else the word "living" means next to nothing, as C. S. Lewis has shown so eloquently.[13]

Scientists who worried about how mental states can possibly emerge from purely physical processes seem to be asking how a mental state arises from something that is already a unity of mental and physical states i.e. living tissue.

The only way to resolve this conceptual tangle is by examining the history of the division between mental and physical states and seeing how the division was forced with many people feeling the strain and ultimately it becomes an impossible one unless of course we are prepared to abandon the word Life altogether by reducing it to a mere abstraction.

Now we are at the point where we can inquire if there might be discernible movement within the dogma that we are biological entities only possessing an emergent property called consciousness with its quality of fleetingness ("a maelstrom of events distributed across the brain").[14] As I have shown, this dogma is strengthening even in the face of conceptual confusion and dismissing of any counter arguments or contrary facts. To put it another way, if a habit of thought is in ascendancy, what gives it strength and endurance, if not reason and argument?

I think there is a discernible movement within the debate and I think that it is this movement that is providing the energy (I better not say "life") to the dogma. This is where we come to Newspeak.

According to Pinker the least controversial feature of the problem of consciousness according to neuroscience is "the idea that our thoughts, sensations, joys and aches consist entirely of physiological activity in the tissues of the brain. Consciousness does not reside in an ethereal soul that uses the brain like a PDA; consciousness is the activity of the brain."[15] This is a succinct expression of the dogma. Within this expression is a clear dismissal of words such as soul as having any reference beyond a material one.

Modern theories can and do become collective representations. Newton's theory of gravity is a good example. We now perceive objects falling passively subject to gravitational forces whereas once they were perceived as actively seeking (falling or rising), ever more eagerly (what we now call accelerating) their desire's fulfilment or natural place relative to the centre of the universe.

Words purportedly having an intangible reference will have no place in the new dogma and will be taken out of the theoretical language altogether. Here is an example of the Newspeak that is already in place. Keep in mind that the speaker is talking about you and me, and indeed, himself:

> "We dream in order to forget." … the brain is like a machine that gets in the groove of connecting its data in certain ways (obsessing or defending or retaining), and that those thinking pathways might not be the most useful for us. But, when we sleep, the brain fires much more randomly. And it is this random scouring for new connections that allows us to loosen certain pathways and create new, potentially useful, ones. Dreaming is a shuffling of old connections that allows us to keep the important connections and erase the inefficient links. A good analogy here is the defragmentation of a computer's hard drive: Dreams are a reordering of connections to streamline the system.[16]

Nowhere to be seen is the pronoun "I". We now use "brain-mind". For people such as Francis Crick (who is quoted in the above passage) dreams hold no meaning at all and simply function to remove unwanted memories. There are of course resistance movements to this theory of dreams as well as to the dismissal of soul, imagination, self, and a host of other words referring to intangible meaning but they pale before the onslaught of MRI scans and the avalanche of evidence showing that just about every mental state is tied to some aspect of the brain.

The theory moves from a theory to a collective representation when ordinary people begin to think of themselves and others in the way the dogma describes, i.e., as brains and stimuli. This thinking slips into the unconscious (should I say "automatic") functioning and we begin to perceive the world that way. Far from Pinker's belief that deep knowledge of our biological roots will open the door to deeper empathy of our neighbour's suffering, we face the prospect of a world of brains bumping against other brains. To gain a vivid glimpse of such a world I can think of no better example than C.S. Lewis' book, That Hideous Strength. Perhaps a passage from that sublime fiction will give the flavour of what may await us if the dominant theory of consciousness becomes a collective representation:

> If you reflect for a moment, said Frost, you will see that your question has no meaning except on the level of the crudest popular thought. Friendship is a chemical phenomenon; so is hatred. Both of them presuppose organisms of our own type. The first step towards intercourse with the macrobes is the realisation that one must go outside the whole world of our subjective

emotions. It is only as you begin to do so that you discover how much of what you mistook for your thoughts was merely a by-product of your blood and nervous tissues … You are to conceive the species as an animal which has discovered how to simplify nutrition and locomotion to such a point that the old complex organs and the old body that contained them are no longer necessary. That large body is therefore to disappear. Only a tenth part of it will be needed to support the brain. The individual is to become all head. The human race is to become all Technocracy.[17]

There are some hopeful signs from within the field of neuroscience, where the dogma is held a little at arm's length. Some concessions are being made towards the mystery of consciousness and its relationship with matter. In the same TIME magazine edition, dedicated to the brain, there is an essay by Scott Haig M.D. It is a sensitive but unsparing portrayal of the last days of a man with terminal cancer which had invaded his brain, replacing much of it with tumour tissue. Against all expectations, his consciousness returned briefly and he could say his goodbyes. Haig was shocked because as a physician he knew the brain just could not be functioning in a way to support speech or even coherence—as he says, "Where that gray stuff grows (the tumour), the brain is just not there." Yet, the patient spoke coherently to his family before dying.

Haig goes on to theorize:

The mind is a uniquely personal domain of thought, dreams, and countless other things, like the will, faith and hope. These fine things are as real as rocks and water, but, like the mind, weightless and invisible, maybe even timeless.[18]

Such brave assertions in the face of the dogma may not be enough to alter the collective representations of the future, maybe not enough to avert Lewis' or Wolfe's glimpse of possible futures, but they are enough to stir the hearts of other resonant souls and that is where I find a realistic hope of a different future from the one offered by the dogma. But how can such a different future arise and find its way into public discourse, finally becoming a collective representation?

In my book, Manifesting Possible Futures, I outline the sequence of steps that develop the participation of an individual with "possible futures" into a collective representation, or shared cultural practice:

a) The individual effort in which an individual's imagination experiences an aspect of an emerging future.

b) The individual becomes a mouthpiece of this future (artist, teacher, author, leader, etc.)

c) The willingness on the part of others to see the future the same way the individual does (e.g. by accepting an artist's work).

d) Through habit what the group is willing to perceive becomes the contours of a new world![19]

We can see this sequence appearing in connection with the dogma I describe above:

Darwin gives us his picture of our origins: the material world appears first, then unconscious life and finally consciousness as a late product of matter

Many take up his picture of the emergence of consciousness from matter and enshrine it in our educational system etc.

Now this picture is so habitually accepted that we have come to perceive the world that way: as a material object that somehow produced human consciousness as an epiphenomenon or emergent property.

There are many authors, artists etc. who, like Thomas Wolfe and C.S. Lewis, give us a glimpse of what horrors await us if the dogma succeeds in becoming a collective representation. Since we are still in a time of transition, or as some would say, chaos, we are in a position to ask if there are other possible futures emerging in the imagination of individuals which could also become a collective representation of ourselves and of the world. In fact there are many, and we can get a good sense of this by watching the mass media in which there is an uncompromising war going on in the domain of competing ideas of our future. It is taking place mainly in politics and economics, since power and money are the engines driving our choices today. There is no more dialogue, thoughtful discussion, or conversation among people today in these domains. Instead we find a "winner takes all" competition in which participants strive to define the issue their way and to eliminate alternative voices as quickly and brutally as possible.

I see in this pervasive dogfight of competing narratives an accelerating competition between individuals each seeking to influence the next set of collective representations. We all seem to believe that individuals can make a decisive contribution to the formation of our species' future, in flagrant contradiction to the prevailing picture of evolution which describes the emerging future with no reference to the actions of individuals at all.

But the domains of money and power come into play at step two of the sequence I outlined above. To get a glimpse of other emerging possible futures we need to explore Step 1 a little more closely. Where are these combatants in the media getting their ideas? To be sure many are getting their ideas from someone else (Step 2) but a few are developing their ideas from within their own imagination (Step 1). It is not easy to trace ideas circulating in the market place back to the individuals who "gave birth" to the idea, but it is possible, as we can see in the case of two ideas that quickly became collective representations—one in the world of public relations, and the other in the world of mathematics and computer science. In each case we can relatively easily see how an original experience in the imagination of an individual is taken up by others and quickly becomes a habit of thought and a commonly perceived reality.[20]

End Notes

[1] Pinker, S. "The Mystery of Consciousness". *TIME*. January 29, 2007, Vol. 169, 5, 59ff.

[2] See my essay *Tarning* in this book for a fuller discussion of how the real appearances of the world come to pass.

[3] Pinker, S. 2007, 62.

[4] Ibid. 62-69.

[5] Ibid. 62.

[6] Wolfe, Tom. Wolfe-Sorry-But-Your-Soul-Just-Died. Othodoxy Today. [Online] 1996. [Cited: 07 23, 2009.] http://orthodoxytoday.org

[7] Ibid.

[8] Ibid.

[9] Pinker, S. 2007, 70.

[10] Wolfe, T. *Sorry but Your Soul Just Died*, 2009.

[11] Pinker, S. 2007, 62.

[12] Freud, S. *Totem and Taboo*. New York : Moffat, Yard and Company, 1919, 207, 231.

[13] Lewis, C. S. *Studies in Words*. Cambridge. Cambridge University Press, 1967.

[14] Pinker, S. 2007, 62.

[15] Ibid.

[16] Simons, I. "The Literary Mind"in *Psychology Today*. 200911

[17] Lewis, C. S. *That Hideous Strength.* London Harper Collins. 1945, 353 ff.

[18] Pinker, S. 2007, 118-9.

[19] Woodcock, John C. *Manifesting Possible Futures*. Bloomington. iUniverse, 2013. Also see my essay, *Tarning*.

[20] See my essay, *Tarning* for this discussion.

DROUGHT or, THE WASTELAND

The aim of this online conference is a "global call for community solutions" to the pressing issue of drought, and contributions may draw from four major disciplines, or areas of knowledge: Science, Business, Politics, and Spirit. The editors encourage a broad range of presentation styles, e.g., interviews, letters, poems, posts, mud, pictures …

This generous "outreach" to the community hints that the time for privileging experts, or authority figures, is over and we are entering an historical moment when we need to tap into something deeper in our being, something wiser, accessible to all.

The *call* for community solutions may be heard as a call to arms, or a call to action: "something must be done!" But, since words convey far more than the surface content of the message, I think it is prudent to develop an ear for the deeper, historical tones that work quietly, even determinatively within the very ordinary words we use to communicate our conscious concerns to one another. This buried or unconscious history in language shapes and informs our real actions in the world much more than does the information we communicate in familiar ways. Because our linguistic heritage lays "hidden", or unconscious, *as the within-ness* of language, we usually only encounter it, at first, as our perceptions of the real world. The world is a real appearance to us, but its appearance, its contours if you like, is an expression of those long-forgotten meanings in our language. What we have "forgotten", through force of habitual usage of words, now appears in front of us, as the contours of the real world, but crucially, as having no felt connection to us anymore.

For example, we easily perceive the parabolic arc that

any object thrown in the air follows in its journey back to earth. But, before Galileo transformed the core meaning of motion, our ancestors perceived a very different trajectory, not parabolic at all, more like a curve for a while, then, straight down. This trajectory was a real appearance to them and we all had to be "taught", through the new concept, how to see the parabolic curve as the new, real appearance of trajectories. As this new perception became a habit, Galileo's revolutionary *concept* of motion that gives rise to the parabolic curve became lost to us and it now lies deep in the history of our language, within the meaning of the commonly used word, motion. We now simply perceive the world as it is: a world in which objects follow parabolic paths.[1]

We can likewise turn our historical imagination to the little examined, but often-used word, "call", as in "a call for community solutions."[2] What historical determinants lie within our unconscious usage of this word, shaping our perceptions of the world, quite independently of our conscious intentions? If we can allow these "roots of meaning" to rise to the surface, how will they affect our discourse re: drought and the present condition of the real world? What action could follow from such an inquiry, i.e. action that matters?

At bottom, "call" surprisingly hides an ancient meaning of screaming, shrieking.[3] Moving "up" through history we also encounter more recent meanings of naming and visitor. Already, from this brief excursion into the historical depths of our being via language, we can see that, through our habitual, unconscious use of the common word "call", in relation to a world condition of drought, psyche is "intending" to alert us to some deeper resonances at work, "behind the scenes as it were", in our perceptions of the world-as-drought.[4] The psyche is thus quite involved in this call to community action, but her involvement may not be quite identical with the understandable sense of urgency we have today, that *we* need to do something, that we need to help the world somehow, in its present plight.

In our use of the word "call", we invoke buried images of shrieking, screaming, naming, and visitor, which can now rise up to the surface of consciousness from the depths of our linguistic being where, if we remain open, they can begin to stain our present consciousness, like an alchemical tincture.

We can now imaginatively ask, for example, *who* is screaming and shrieking, without needing to literalize the question by that old habit of thought, or trope—the inner/outer disjunction. If we do succumb to the trope, then we can only conclude that we humans are literally shrieking or screaming, or alternatively, that the world is poetically "screaming" for our help. This familiar move betrays psychic being, which is no longer concerned with the truth of such disjunctions as inner/outer, as Nietzsche demonstrates so forcefully in his opus.[5]

To serve psyche today, it is more important that we *receive* the shrieking and screaming as it comes to us from our and the world's mutual depths of being. This may be in fact what we are here to do, as Rilke teaches through the example of his own life:

> Since I still don't know enough about pain,
> This terrible darkness makes me small.
> If it's you, though—
> press down hard on me, break in
> that I may know the weight of your hand,
> and you the fullness of my cry.[6]

Or, as he says further on:

> Are we, perhaps, here just for saying: House,
> Bridge, Fountain, Gate, Jug, Olive tree, Window,—
> Possibly: Pillar, Tower? … But for saying, remember,
> Oh, for such saying as never the things themselves
> Hoped so intensely to be.[7]

Can we resonate with the screaming and shrieking long enough to hear its name, as it names itself to us, in the way that a visitor would introduce herself?

I had a dream recently in which a visitor called at my door. Children, light-hearted and laughing, accompanied it. This visitor rendered me mute. I could not name it. It has a shape of a cat's head that morphs into the body of a cassowary, an Australian bird from the emu family. This strange being came into my home and washed its face in a fountain. It was friendly and seemed to get what it wanted from our meeting. After the dream, I am still mute and must therefore wait until my marvelous visitor begins to speak through me, as its possible mouthpiece. It is not up to me to name it as if it belongs to my familiar world.

This visitor *could* appear to me only after decades of my dwelling in the "screaming and shrieking", following its first appearance in my life, at a time when I was *living the drought*, the kind of wasteland that T. S. Eliot's poem knows: [8]

> What are the roots that clutch, what branches grow
> Out of this stony rubbish? Son of man,
> You cannot say, or guess, for you know only
> A heap of broken images, where the sun beats,
> And the dead tree gives no shelter, the cricket no relief,
> And the dry stone no sound of water. Only
> There is shadow under this red rock,

(Come in under the shadow of this red rock),
And I will show you something different from either
Your shadow at morning striding behind you
Or your shadow at evening rising to meet you;
I will show you fear in a handful of dust.[9]

While we normally think that something has to be done to the wasteland in order to rescue it, or nourish it, I learned that the wasteland itself is the "place" of its own "cure", if we can stay long enough within it. And so, from within the drought came this life-changing, powerful, dream-vision:

I am working at a thermonuclear facility along with others. It is the central facility of our society. It is regulated and master-minded by a central computer, much like HAL in '2001', even to the detail of the red eye with which we could communicate. This computer is female. Everybody thought of her as an IT! In contrast I would look into her eye and talk to her, subject to subject, with love.

In other words, the feminine regulating principle which is the glue of society, by relating all parts to one another and to the whole has become an IT! But my response alone is not enough. Slowly the lack of relatedness begins to drive her mad with grief. At first, this madness showed up as an increasing, dangerous autonomy in the operation of the objects associated with the facility (society)—elevators going sideways, doors opening and shutting autonomously, etc. Then people began to harm one another in various ways until the social system became frayed and anarchy increased, with civilization and its values losing cohesion and crumbling.

I find myself in a garbage dump, near the central facility. Some abandoned children give me a gun to kill them. I take it away from them. A vagabond is sitting in an abandoned car, sewing a boot for the coming (nuclear?) winter. He also used to work in the facility, he said. A sick woman careens by. A man tries to take his twin boys up a tower.

Then I am standing at the centre of the facility. It is Ground Zero. A large cleared area of gray sand and dirt with concentric rings, like a target, radiating from the centre. The ground is slightly raised at the centre, like a discus, sloping away to the edges. I sense that she is going to explode. I am right at the epicentre. She is going to destroy us all and this means herself in an apocalypse of rage-despair, loathing, hate, and grief because of our stupidity. I must get away from the epicentre now. I sprint across the field, down the slight incline to the periphery of the field and sprawl prone, with my head facing the centre, just as she explodes. The wind starts from the centre and blows out (in contrast to the natural phenomenon which sucks up). It begins as a breeze, increasing in strength and intensity until it becomes an unbearable shriek. Lying face down, I am sheltered by the slope as the wind rips over my back. But I mustn't raise my head at all—a few inches of protection and that's it! Then I know the shriek is hers.

I 'see' her standing at the centre, and a poem bursts spontaneously out of me as I record the experience:

goddess
flowing
in her agony
awesome!
incomparable grief and rage
divine suffering
excruciating pain
such terrible agony
beauty, sublime beauty
how is love possible?
yet this is what i feel

A bubble of calm forms around me while the storm of destruction rages on outside. She is with me in a form that

I can talk to, personally. Then the bubble collapses and the wind/goddess shrieks again. Gradually it dissipates and as I turn over, feeling its last tendrils whip at my clothes, I find myself tumbling out of this apocalyptic scene into a city street, the everyday world of my daily life. I have been returned from a visionary place to my ordinary life.

Then, I wake up.

This self-presentation of reality did indeed stain my being, like an alchemical tincture. I was brought to edge of suicide, over subsequent months. "Her" screaming and shrieking *became* mine, as it already was from the start, i.e., existing in the depths of being, beyond "mine" and "yours", beyond "inner" and "outer". How could I stand the given knowledge that Being itself, in the form of the goddess, has been consigned to oblivion, abandoned, for over 3000 years by the cultural encrustation that privileges the human subject and centuries-long imposition of its various "worldviews" *on* Being? The goddess, ignored for so long, is now destroying that which she loves and in so doing, destroys herself. This knowledge "pressed down hard upon me," as Rilke says, and her rage-despair became the "fullness of my cry."

Yet the very same dreadful terror carries the "miraculous cure" within it. I was given a poem that worked performatively on me. "Incomparable grief and rage", if endured by the human recipient, will transform into love, and indeed did so, as I feverishly wrote with increasing astonishment. The *poesis* itself generated love from the depths of rage-despair, all within the human heart.

The "call" begins with shrieking and screaming, and reveals, decades later, an as-yet unnamed friendly visitor who calls upon me. Although this strange and wonderful being did not offer up a name, I am struck by the fact that it came as an animal figure. I can presently only conceive of this marvel in terms of a complex image: a cat's head and a cassowary's body. This presentation means that I do not yet know the "speech" of this (way of) being, coming to us from within the despair of the drought or nuclear wasteland.

My "visitor" dream shows there is a clear affinity between this new way of "animal being" and fountains of water. Does this suggest that the drought is brought to an end when we can politely receive the unknown visitor, without imposing yet another "worldview" on its presence? Can we become more animal-like, in the way that van der Post advises, concerning bush manners— knowing how to comport ourselves in the face of the unknown, friendly, but possibly dangerous (cassowaries have a lethal kick) "animal" presence?[10]

We are not only faced with literal droughts *in* the world; we are critically facing a world appearing *as* drought—a waterless wasteland, now filled only with a self-destructive rage-despair. The appearance of the strange "animal" visitor coincides with the appearance of a fountain—the end of the drought, if this strange being can be received as such by us.

We are presently faced with the end of one entire way of being, a way that has dominated for 3000 years, and the "call" heralds a new way of being. One of its "faces" is that of my dream visitor. To receive this visitor and end the drought is a task that begins with hearing and receiving the abyssal depths of our historical being, in the form of shrieks and screams—the agony of 3000 years of consignment to oblivion. If we can endure, suffer this rage-despair, as it works its will on us, then love may be born in our hearts, the kind of love that can prepare us to receive the next manifestation of being, the strange and wonderful "animal" presence. If we can restrain the Adamic impulse to *impose* a name on this wonderful being, then it may, in time, name itself to us, and in so doing … name us!

Returning now to the call for community solutions, what effective action may follow when the psychic determinants of our perceptions are brought into relationship to our conscious concerns? There is no compulsion to include *psychic* being as a factor in any analysis of our modern predicament. Most disciplines in fact proceed from a very different *a priori*. They assume that our present set of real appearances—a solid world exterior to human consciousness, having no consciousness of its own—has been the only one for all time. The corollary to this stance is that we humans are solely responsible for our present crisis and its solution—there is only us *human* beings![11]

Accepting *psychic* being, distinguished from *human* being, as an *a priori*, is a choice and commitment, usually based on some convincing experience of the reality of the psyche, and not simply an ideological choice, based on personal preference. Once the commitment is made, we become open to what psyche may teach us in regards to the real world's *being* and our place in it. My experiences with psychic reality have taught me, for example, that the drought, from psyche's point of view, though disturbingly real, is not simply some event exterior to me, and equally, "drought" is not simply a projected quality of my personal psychological situation onto the exterior world. Drought, or the wasteland, is the condition of the real world in its present *being*, at a depth shared by all of us. Once the human being goes to those depths and becomes a mouthpiece for the rage-despair that lies there, then the world's being may "speak" through, and *as*, its human representative. Such "speech" may take the form of "art", new modes of discourse, or cultural forms that can reflect a new human-world configuration.[12] As this new configuration manifests through the creative efforts of many individuals, a correspondingly new set of real appearance will arise, an inceptive moment that, as Heidegger says, will inaugurate an entirely new history.

End Notes

[1] Bortoft, H. *The Wholeness of Nature*. Aurora. Lindisfarne Books, 1996.

[2] The term, "historical imagination" is from Owen Barfield and is a method of participating with past consciousnesses.

[3] Old Norse kalla "to cry loudly;" Proto-Indo-European base *gol- "to scream, shriek." From WordBook. 2012.

[4] From the psyche's point of view, the "past" means "psychic depth", or the depths of our being.

[5] Paul de Man, reading Nietzsche, asks: "are the axioms of logic adequate to reality or are they a means and measure for us *create* the real …" de Man, P. (1979). *Allegories of Reading*. New Haven. Yale University Press, 120.

[6] Rilke, R. *Book of Hours*. Barrows, A. & Macy, J. (Trs). New York. Riverhead Books, 1996.

[7] Rilke, R. "The Ninth Elegy" in *Duino Elegies*. Leishman & Spender, S. (Trs). New York. Norton, 1967.

[8] For a fuller account of this period of my life, see Woodcock, J. C. *The Imperative*. CreateSpace, 2015.

[9] Eliot, T. S. *The Wasteland.*

[10] "Human beings ... are so deficient in the essentials of bush education such as having a proper sense of smell and hearing ..." From van der Post, L. *A Story Like The Wind.* New York. Morrow, 1978.

[11] Our present cultural practices reflect a definition of human beings as isolated centres of consciousness over and against a material world whose meaning can only be *posited* by these centres of authority—if *we* don't endow the world with this or that "world view" then the world holds no meaning at all.

[12] My book, Oblivion of Being, narrates a story of three friends who, following an inceptive moment, engage in the effort of developing a new cultural form that can reflect a transformation in the definition of the human being and world.

PARTICIPATORY consciousness

PREFACE

This essay arose from my personal experience of a life-changing transformation in consciousness, which lasted over twenty years. Like other individuals who also have been subjected to the emergence of an essentially new personality from an old one, I sought to "locate" his experience within the context of a theory of the evolution of consciousness. My discovery of a *participatory consciousness* became the key to overcoming the "Cartesian" split between modern consciousness and nature and led to the work of Owen Barfield who is a pioneer in the study of the evolution of consciousness through the history of language. I also separately studied the work of C.G. Jung who explored the evolution of consciousness through investigations into the nature of the human soul or psyche. In linking my personal experiences to the works of these authors I discovered that the separate disciplines of philology and depth psychology in fact belong together as one discipline, which can form a solid theoretical basis for the task of assisting the birth of participatory consciousness out of our modern state of alienation.

INTRODUCTION

I was walking along to the final class I would ever teach at Antioch University. I passed some trees where I heard a young crow cawing loudly. It was early summer so I assumed he was calling for his mother to feed him. I watched for a while and then moved on, intent on getting to class. The little crow hopped from tree to tree in the street along with me. I slowly grew interested enough in his behaviour to forget that I was moving until I jammed my knee into the nearest fire hydrant that could find its way towards me.

OK OK I'll watch where I'm going! But the little bird continued along with me. So I stopped, and decided to experiment. I walked back along where I had come. He followed me. I resumed my way towards school and so did he, cawing loudly and insistently. When I stopped, he stopped, never ceasing his call. I went inside a building for a while and there he was waiting for me when I came out, resuming his flight along side, cawing as I made my way to class. By now it HAD become "he was following me and was calling to me." The experience had quite definitely become that now.

I felt a peculiar feeling, a tension growing in my belly as we went on. I ducked into a shop to get him some food but he ignored it, perching on a building ledge cawing at me. He even ignored the food that his mother did eventually bring to him, preferring it seemed, to call at me. I started to gather a strong feeling that something was urgent in this, that I was not getting it, that he was trying to get something through to me and I had yet to get it. I was starting to get quite nervous and a heightened sense of alertness gathered. I still had thirty minutes before class so I quickly went upstairs to my room and turned all the lights off so that I could crawl into a corner and see what would happen next. Well, I immediately looked out the window and there he was, my little crow, calling me, his whole body opened to the effort of … what? I could no longer shake the conviction that he was trying to get something through to me and that I needed to make an effort to find a way to reach him to understand him.

Obviously I was not going to do it with my ego, which

had up to now led the way. I had to find another place where we could communicate ... just had to! I was fully engaged now. I felt an imperative not to leave this experience without success. My little crow's urgent cries were unnerving me. I felt highly attuned to him.

I let go. Immediately I recalled a passing moment, earlier in the day:

> I am walking to my office when I pass a second hand bookstore. An artist is usually parked just outside in his customary place where he copies famous paintings onto his canvas. However, it is not him this time. Another artist is there painting birds, not copying them, but drawing from his own interior instead. I pause. He is in casual conversation with an elderly lady, a tourist, so I fancy. He tells her, and, by the subtle method of eavesdropping while pretending to do something else, he also tells me, that birds have to cock their heads side by side in order to get a whole picture of something. He goes on to say that birds, having eyes opposed, one on each side of their head cannot form a whole picture of what they see that way. They see two distinct pictures that cannot be made into a whole.

As this memory surfaced, another was quickly released. In Melville's book, *Moby Dick* there is a passage where Melville describes the whale's head, with its little eyes: "... the whale, therefore, must see one distinct picture on this side and another distinct picture on that side; while all between must be profound darkness and nothingness to him."[1]

Then he poses a question: whether the whale can, simultaneously, attentively examine two distinct prospects, one on each side of him. He notes that whales sometimes behave as if they are reacting helplessly to two distinct events which are acting upon them through their diametrically opposed eyes.

From there I remembered a puzzling passage I had read in Jung's Zarathustra Lectures, where he equates the symbol of the eagle with the brain of man.[2] The wings correspond to the two halves of the brain while the body corresponds to the commissure, where the two halves meet and communicate with one another. Jung refers to this organ as the seat of consciousness, where the naive mind experiences a oneness, never realizing or feeling at all the two halves on either side of that seat.

Even now as I write, yet another memory is released. I saw a film long ago in an undergraduate psychology class where experiments were carried out on the consciousness of people who had had the two halves of the brain separated by surgery. They could function perfectly well except in circumstances where contradictions arose. It seemed that each half carried on as if it had absolutely no knowledge of the other half at all.

As these memories were released I began to ask whether there was something about all this that I needed to get. What would the bird need from the human that is connected to the bird structure of the eye and brain, as well as the whale's and the human's? Does he need me as the human to do something that he cannot do? Does he sense the urgency, the imperative of getting it done but needs the human representative to carry it out? I felt and still feel very disinclined to treat this experience as a projective field in which I might explore a purely human psychic matter such as the bird representing some aspect of my human psyche etc. Rather it feels to me to be the world calling me through the mouth of this little crow, seeking to connect with me on a matter of vital urgency, requiring my immediate attention.

I regard the place where I found those memories as precisely that threshold where the human, the animal and the world meet and can speak the same language. It is in this sacred place where Creation can meet and speak to its human representative.

Owen Barfield refers to such startling experiences as *final participation*, a term he uses to name the next step in the evolution of consciousness.[3] Final participation follows the current split between human and world, a split that has been variously described by many people today. But few have explored the evolution of consciousness with the depth and precision of Owen Barfield. It was left to him to show that the "Cartesian" split is not an aberration to be corrected. Rather, he shows that our current devastating dissociation from nature and the body is a necessary evolutionary pre-condition for what may follow—final participation!

Barfield's contribution to the study of the evolution of consciousness and his revolutionary challenge to the Darwinian view of evolution is gaining attention today but there is another contribution he has made that has not been stressed, yet which seems to me to be equally significant to our culture. In drawing his conclusions about the evolution of consciousness from a study of language, Barfield in effect has rejoined two disciplines that were sundered at the moment of their birth: philology and psychology.

This essay is a small attempt to show how Barfield achieved this union.

Barfield's Historical Approach to Language

In his book, History in English Words, Barfield begins to

describe his premise and his methodology:

> (L)anguage has preserved for us the inner, living history of man's soul. It reveals the evolution of consciousness. . . . in order to excavate the information which is buried in a word we must have the means to ascertain its history.[4]

The means of ascertaining the history of a word was found in the ground-breaking discoveries of philology in Europe from the 18th century onwards. Campbell describes it this way:

> As early as 1767 a French Jesuit in India, Father Coeurdoux, had observed that Sanskrit and Latin were remarkably alike. Sir William Jones (1746-1794)—the West's first considerable Sanskritist, judge of the supreme court of judicature at Calcutta, and founder of the Bengal Asiatic Society—was the next to observe the relationship, and from a comparative study of the grammatical structures of Latin, Greek, and Sanskrit concluded that all three had "sprung," as he phrased it, "from some common source, which perhaps no longer exists." Franz Bopp (1791-1867), published in 1816 a comparative study of the Sanskrit, Greek, Latin, Persian, and Germanic systems of conjugation. And finally, by the middle of the century it was perfectly clear that a prodigious distribution of closely related tongues could be identified over the greater part of the civilized world: a single, broadly scattered family of languages that must have sprung from a single source.[5]

So many languages were now traceable to a single imagined source called the Indo-European or Aryan parent language. This is the means of tracing the history of language that Barfield was able to use as a tool to reach his conclusions regarding the evolution of consciousness. But there is much more to his methodology than this! In his early research into the power of figurative words to change consciousness,

Barfield paid particular attention to the phenomenology of metaphor. He noticed how our experience of metaphor changes over time:

First he studied how meaning comes into language and the world. When a speaker tries to say something that possibly had not been said before, he would express it as an image which contained elements already known, but whose connotation went beyond those known elements. In this way, meaning would be extended into life and culture would be enriched. Barfield calls this a figurative expression. He uses the example of the word *focus*, which Kepler used to describe the geometry of ellipses. This word is now collective in meaning but began with Kepler extending the meaning of the Latin word, which referred to the hearth of a home.[6]

Barfield noticed that over time with much usage, a fresh figurative expression becomes a trope i.e. a conventional expression that has lost the image.

He also noticed that when he studied an older language, which still expressed figuratively, he experienced the same pleasure as with a metaphor before it becomes a trope, or even a cliché.

These three aspects of Barfield's relatively simple phenomenological research form the basis of his methodology. They reveal startling conclusions regarding the evolution of consciousness and its challenge to the Darwinian-based assumptions about the relationship between mind and matter.

Barfield calls his methodology "The Semantic Approach to History" and I believe it qualifies as an original contribution to knowledge in which philology and depth psychology once again are united after being prematurely divided. As Lockhart says:

> It is interesting to me that the greatest period of work in the etymology of language, what we might call a study of the unconscious depths of language, also occurred in the latter part of the nineteenth century (as did Psychoanalysis). Language was beginning to discover its origins at about the same time as the psyche was concerned with its origins. But the two great sciences etymology and psychology, did not come together. For the most part those individuals studying the depths of language were resistant to psychology and psychoanalysis, while those psychologists who did study language were generally resistant to depth psychology. Depth psychologists rarely have ventured into the psychology of language.[7]

A Depth Psychological Approach to Language

In 1983, Jungian Analyst Russell Lockhart wrote a remarkable book called *Words as Eggs*. The title essay describes the birth of his method of researching the interiority of words, which he calls *etymological fantasy*. Essentially it is the same methodology as Barfield's, arrived at from the field of depth psychology. Lockhart describes his method this way:

> I decided to start by looking up each of the major words in my dream: word, egg, life, birth. I decided, too, that since I was to enter this activity in something other than a utilitarian spirit, I would pay strict attention to what happened to me under the stimulus of the word. If the word were to induce an imaginative reaction, then I would have to be ready to follow it. [8]

This is exactly the same kind of research as Barfield's in which he (Barfield) follows what he calls "pleasure". Both researchers start with the history of the word but neither follow the trail into history with a utilitarian spirit. Rather each seeks to follow the trail to the "interiority of the word".

Lockhart:

> I realized that I couldn't go further until I determined what the dictionary was doing with this word symbol. So I went to the word and asked it what it meant. And the first thing it said was: "a material used to represent something invisible." I was quite literally shocked by this. It was not just a sign or token but, clearly, a word was a materiality representing something invisible. This excited me because a word could represent something invisible in a meaning, and that seemed very connected to my dream of words as eggs. After all, what is inside the egg is hidden, invisible, not seen. This symbol idea pointed to something inside, an interiority of some kind. I had now the image of words speaking to me.[9]

Barfield:

> More particularly it (i.e. pleasure) can be aroused by a language which is at an earlier stage of development than the one that is our own, because it is the nature of language to grow less figurative, less and less couched in terms of imagery, as it grows older. We notice, we relish figurative quality in older language, and we experience this figurative element in the same way that we experience a metaphor before it has faded or before it has become fossilised. That is also the way in which we experience those new metaphors which poets make for us. But it does not follow from this (and this is where most of the philologists of the 19th Century and the early Twenties have really made their mistake) it does not follow from this that that figurative element, that presence of living imagery, that we find in earlier language was made, invented, created by the individual genius of a poet. On the contrary, it couldn't have been. It was simply there in the language as

such; it was a 'given' kind of meaning, a 'given' kind of imagery.

Both Barfield and Lockhart engage in a method of research into the history of words that seeks to connect with the interiority of the word i.e. *its* imagination, not their own subjective imaginations. The method moves from dry literal meanings towards uncovering the images locked within the shell of the word. The path followed is determined by those connections that bring pleasure, i.e. both researchers follow connections that are spontaneously made through erotic arousal produced by the release of images into their consciousness during the course of research. It is a most difficult form of research since the ego of the researcher must take a back seat to the workings of two other principles described by Lockhart as the interactions between Eros and Psyche, which bring pleasure and connectedness in the form of an image. Barfield, who openly declares his debt to Rudolph Steiner would surely have been familiar with Steiner's work on the phenomenology of the waking soul in which the interactions between love and desire are described as the "cause" of the formation of images.

It is the idea that words have their own interiority that is so crucial to Barfield's and Lockhart's research methodology and conclusions. Lockhart expresses this idea as the presentational psyche in his own development of the work of C.G. Jung, who introduced terms such as the objective psyche and the collective unconscious, and that of artists such as the Irish poet AE.[10] This idea is fast gaining currency in the field of depth psychology and beyond, under the name of Sophianic wisdom.

The spontaneous release of image from the word itself, into the consciousness of the researcher, connotes the interiority of language, as both Lockhart and Barfield describe. The image self-presents and as such is the self-expression of nature. As Barfield says, "the presence of living imagery . . . was simply there in the language as such; it was a 'given' kind of meaning, a 'given' kind of imagery."[11]

As an example of Barfield's method of seeking to release the image from the word, I can turn to his vivid description of the Aryans. In one small piece of his description he begins his research by a philological exploration of the word "bed" and finds that it is connected to a Latin stem, "fod". This connection releases a vivid image in Barfield of "a roof and walls of wood and wattles, bounding a dark interior crowded with human beings and possibly some cattle . . ." etc. Thus Barfield discovered the interiority of the word "bed."[12]

Barfield's "Participation" & Depth Psychology

From Barfield's study of the history of language, which reveals the innate interiority of language he draws his revolutionary conclusion concerning the consciousness of our ancestors, which he calls original participation:

> If the figurative, or let's say the imaginal, meaning in the earliest words was really "given", and was not something added to them by an individual speaker (which is what happens when a metaphor is invented), then there must have been going on, not only a different kind of thinking but a different kind of perceiving. The picture quality, the given meanings must have been present not only in the perceiver but also in what he perceived; it must have been present in fact in the world about him. There must have been a kind of participation between perceiver and perceived, between man and nature. That is something we

no longer experience, only get an occasional glimpse of its quality through the creative imagination of a modem painter or poet.

If you can grant this, you see language as originating in that participation, so that in the earliest stages of all it would have to be described as nature speaking through man, rather than man speaking about nature; and you see the subsequent development of language as evincing the gradual diminution of that participation as time went on.[13]

His conclusion is that consciousness began in a kind of original participation with nature in which the interiority of nature is ontologically prior to the consciousness of the human being. In original participation the human being has no subjective consciousness but rather, is a vessel through which nature expresses her interiority. Barfield's idea of participation shows how close philology and depth psychology really are, when compared with Jung's central notions of the collective unconscious and *participation mystique*, a term he used heavily, having borrowed it from anthropology.

Barfield arrives at his conclusion of an original participation of the human being and nature by including a kind of structural analysis of the phenomenon he is examining. In other words, he links structures of consciousness with possibilities of language. For example, he notes that when we use language that involves thinking about phenomena, then this implies that, "we must necessarily be aware of ourselves (that is, of the self which is doing the thinking) as sharply and clearly detached from the thing thought about."

This example shows the subtle way in which Barfield links structures of consciousness with language forms and his concept of "participation" is crucial to this link.

One way he defines it is as "of self and not-self identified in the same moment of experience". This formulation shows vividly the close connections between psychology and philology.

Original participation is therefore a term Barfield uses to name an extra-sensory link between the percipient and the representations. This implies not only that we think differently, but also that the phenomena (collective representations) are different. He goes on to say that we never have lost our participation in the phenomenon but that we do so today unconsciously. This finding is startlingly close to those of depth psychology and object-relations psychology, particularly to Jung's idea of the objective psyche or collective unconscious.

In considering Jung, Barfield charges him with having a residue of unresolved positivism (RUP) in his writings about the evolution of consciousness. By this derogatory term, he is criticizing those authors who may subscribe to a theory that the human being and the world are not fundamentally separate. However, their actual writings betray the fact that the authors do not really believe their own theory, i.e. they still write as if humans and the world are fundamentally separate.

> Jung is very ambiguous. There are passages in Jung where he very definitely does show that he has this residue of unresolved positivism. He calls the unconscious "collective," and he says also that it is a residuum of innumerable racial memories or something like that. He's thinking of the whole historical series of individual human beings as collecting up the collective unconscious.
>
> The collective unconscious is really understood only if you see it not as something which arose out of the aggregation of a number of experiences had by individual

human beings but as something out of which the human individual and his physical body originally arose. There are other passages in Jung where he does speak of archetypes as if he meant it that way. But I accuse him of RUP because more often he speaks in the other way.[14]

I believe this justified criticism exposes the conflict in Jung as he tried to pour his profound mystical sense of the psyche being ontologically prior to human subjectivity into the vessel of science that was available to him at the time. He was very concerned with being accepted in the terms of the day i.e. science based as it is on logical positivism. So, for example, he describes the evolution of consciousness in terms of the idea of projection and its withdrawal which theory also surely earns the label of unresolved positivism.

Such an approach demonstrates how a modern mind can read into the "past" imposing its structure of consciousness on the past. For example, it is impossible to talk about projection unless the structure of consciousness is such that self and world are already divided. We cannot assume that about our ancestors so it makes no sense to talk of their "projecting" onto the environment.

Yet, Jung's most fundamental discoveries and convictions place him very close to Barfield in essence:

Shall we, for the moment at least, venture the hypothesis that the primitive belief in arbitrary powers is justified by the facts and not merely from a psychological point of view? This sounds alarming, but I have no intention of jumping from the frying-pan into the fire and trying to prove that witchcraft actually exists. I wish only to consider the conclusions to which we shall be led if we follow primitive man in supposing that all light comes from the sun, that things are beautiful in themselves and that a human part-soul is a leopard. In doing this we accept the primitive idea of mana. According to this idea, the beautiful moves us, and it is not we who create beauty. A certain person is a devil—we have not projected our own evil upon him and in this way made a devil out of him. There are people—mana personalities—who are impressive in their own right, and in no way thanks to our imagination. The mana conception has it that there exists something like a widely distributed force in the external world that produces all those effects which are out of the common. Everything that exists, acts, for otherwise it would not be actual. It is only actual thanks to its inherent energy. Being is a field of force. The primitive mana conception, as we can see, is of the nature of a crude theory of energy.

So far we can easily follow this primitive idea. The difficulty arises when we try to carry its implications further, for they reverse the process of psychic projection of which I have spoken. These implications are as follows: it is not my imagination or my awe that makes a sorcerer of the medicine-man; on the contrary, he is a sorcerer and projects his magical powers upon me. Ghosts are not hallucinations of my mind, but appear to me of their own volition. Although such statements are logical derivatives of the mana idea, we hesitate to accept them and begin to look around us for our comfortable theory of psychic projection. The question is nothing less than this: does the psychic in general—that is, the spirit, or the unconscious— arise in us; or is the psyche, in the early stages of consciousness, actually outside us in the form of arbitrary powers with intentions of their own, and does it gradually come to take its place within us in the course of psychic development? Were the dissociated psychic contents—to use our modern terms—ever parts of the psyches of individuals, or were they rather from the beginning psychic entities existing in themselves according to the primitive view as ghosts, ancestral spirits and the like? Were they only by degrees embodied by man in the course of development, so that they gradually constituted in him that world which we now call the psyche?[15]

This description of the collective unconscious by Jung seems to me to be very close to Barfield's statement that "[i]t becomes clear that, both ontogenetically and phylogenetically, subjectivity is never something that was developed out of nothing at some point of space, but is a form of consciousness that has contracted from the periphery into individual centers."[16]

So far I am suggesting that the concept of participation is very close to Jung's concept of the poorly named collective unconscious or his idea of the objective psyche. Related to these are the anthropological concept of *participation mystique* and the object-relations concept of projective identification.

I believe that my experience with my little crow is an example of participation but I would like to amplify the phenomenology here. In order to do so adequately, I need to introduce some terms that are essential to any description of participation. The first aspect to note is that our participation with nature has never ceased. Only our awareness of our participation has ceased. As Barfield says: ". . . we do, in fact, still participate in the phenomena, though for the most part we do so unconsciously. *We* can only remind ourselves of that participation by beta-thinking and we forget it as soon as we leave off."[17] As our subjectivity became more concentrated, our awareness of our participation lessened. This fact seems to offer an important historical reason for the necessity of the "discovery" of the unconscious since the language of the unconscious allows us to speak about our participation once more, through, as Barfield says, beta-thinking, which is a kind of thinking about our "collective representations", a term Barfield uses to name what we collectively and ordinarily call real. In thinking about these collective representations, we have found that something of ourselves is inevitably contained in our perceptions of our collective representations. This idea is expressed in phenomenology as intentionality; in Kantian thought as categories; in Jungian thought as participation mystique (borrowed from Levy-Bruhl), or unconscious identity; in object relations theory as projective identification.

Barfield notes that although beta thinking can demonstrate conceptually our participation to us, we still remain unavailable to an actual experience of that participation. To put it in terms of depth psychology, it remains unconscious. For modern consciousness, the actual experience of nature is not participatory but disjunctive. We connect in consciousness with nature only through our senses. This connection leaves nature as an object to be looked "onto" rather than "into".

For us to move from beta thinking to an actual experience of participation, we would need to have an experience of conscious figuration rather than unconscious figuration. Barfield means by "figuration" the creative aspect in us that makes sensations into objects; in other words that aspect in us that transforms the impressions of the sense organs into perception of the known world. This formulation is predicated on Barfield's knowledge and acceptance of the split existing today between our ordinary familiar world of experience and the world discovered by science. In fact, Barfield's opus may be seen as a brilliant attempt to bridge this gap. His notion of figuration is a logical consequence of the split.

C.G. Jung found a similar notion, based on his understanding of the split. He called the creative factor in human beings the archetype, which I believe corresponds very closely to the idea of figuration. From Jung's point of view, archetypes are the way we perceive the world; they are the image making capacity of the collective unconscious or objective psyche. They result in our collective representations, which term as I said refers to our ordinary world of experience. Barfield's sense of conscious figuration corresponds with Jung's idea of an experience of an archetype—an experience he describes closely in many of his works.

With these terms introduced now, I can proceed to the phenomenon of participation. Today we participate in the world, as we always have but we remain unconscious of that participation. As Barfield points out, drawing from the work of Levy-Bruhl and Durkheim, our ancestors were quite conscious of their participation. They had a super-sensory awareness of the participation with no subjectivity involved. The term that best captures this experience is *mana*, which Jung describes this way:

> The mana conception has it that there exists something like a widely distributed force in the external world that produces all these effects which are out of the common. Everything that exists acts, for otherwise it would not be natural. It is only actual thanks to its inherent energy. Being is a field of force. The primitive mana conception, as we can see, is of the nature of a crude theory of energy.[18]

The crucial detail of a lack of subjectivity sharply distinguishes our ancestors' perceptions from our own today. They cannot be said to imagine, as we do. So, language that suggests they perceive magic properties in objects is incorrect because such language presupposes a subject-object differentiation.

Jung offers a descriptive report of original participation or participation mystique here:

> Among such (primitive) people, whose consciousness is at a different level of development from ours, the "soul" (or psyche) is not felt to be a unit. Many primitives assume that a man has a "bush soul" as well as his own, and that this bush soul is incarnate in a wild animal or a tree, with which the human individual has some kind of psychic identity. This is what the distinguished French ethnologist Lucien Levy-Bruhl called a "mystical participation." He later retracted this term under pressure of adverse criticism, but I believe that his critics were wrong. It is a well-known psychological fact that an individual may have such an unconscious identity with some other person or object.
>
> This identity takes a variety of forms among primitives. If the bush soul is that of an animal, the animal itself is considered as some sort of brother to the man. A man whose brother is a crocodile, for instance, is supposed to be safe when swimming a crocodile-infested river. If the bush soul is a tree, the tree is presumed to have something like parental authority over the individual concerned. In both cases an injury to the bush soul is interpreted as an injury to the man.[19]

But how can we now, today get inside such an uncanny world in which objects are "stopping-places of *mana*" and in which a super-sensory link exists, and is perceived between the human and the world? It is easy enough to give reports about original participation as Jung and Barfield do as well as the anthropologists. But to get inside it, to release the essence of the experience is daunting because of the problem of having a totally different consciousness today, one that is dissociated from nature. However, there is a way available to the Western modern mind, based on Barfield's rightful claim that we have never stopped participating with nature and that we are moving towards doing so once more: "Consequently if our participation, having been first understood and accepted, by beta-thinking, as a fact, should then become a conscious experience, it would have to take the form of conscious (instead of, as now, unconscious) figuration."[20]

He calls this form of participation, final participation, since it is his thesis that Western European consciousness is developing towards this form. Thus, in final participation we may approach an experience of original participation. In other words, whereas our ancestors were simply in original participation, we may experience consciously the same kind of participation in nature and the world, while remaining aware of our separateness. This therefore is the only way in which we may approach the strange and uncanny world of original participation.

Conclusion

Although Barfield identifies the tendency towards final participation in the evolution of consciousness, we are by no means there yet and so to conclude, I want to ask: what are the kinds of experiences that are available to us today which could herald or hint at final participation?

I believe my experience with the little crow is such a moment when participation became conscious. In Jungian terms I experienced a synchronicity, a phenomenon discovered and studied extensively by Jung, which has since gathered an increasing interest across the sciences and humanities.

Synchronicity is a phenomenon marked by a collapse of the usual subject-object distinction with the corresponding inner-outer distinction but ego-consciousness remains. It is always accompanied by a shock, thus sharply distinguishing the experience from ordinary coincidences. It operates through our emotions, not our ordinary consciousness, and thus *pulls* on us, the experience being one of the sudden presence of *otherness*, as Otto describes so well.[21] We cannot interpret it in terms of what is already known, and thus we feel led into the unknown future. In a moment of synchronicity we are once again participating in the sense that Barfield means. We become aware of our participation in the world-as-living-subject. We involuntarily respond to the *otherness* of the world, which once again assumes interiority, becoming a living presence that reduces the human to a far more humble station than what we are used to today. A gasp! A recoil! A fascination! A wonderment! It is phenomenologically the same world as our ancestors, except that ego-consciousness, the subjective consciousness remains intact. And, like our ancestors, what becomes important assumes a radically different shape than what we are accustomed to. A shoe can frighten the wits out of us; a mundane shop sign can open us to wonder and a gesture can become filled with significance. At the same time, we can (unlike our ancestors) perceive their ordinariness with our subjectivity and through our senses.

In comparison with Jung's fertile concept of synchronicity Barfield offers a stimulating description of the process by which meaning changes in culture. It involves a process of participation, which he describes in terms of the interaction between "speaker's meaning" and "lexical meaning."

> The more common a word is and the simpler its meaning, the bolder very likely is the original thought which it contains and the more intense the intellectual or poetic effort which went to its making. Thus, the word quality is used by most educated people every day of their lives, yet in order that we should have this simple word Plato had to make the tremendous effort (it is one of the most exhausting which man is called on to exert) of turning a vague feeling into a clear thought.
>
> He invented the new word 'poiotes', 'what-ness', as we might say, or 'of-what-kind-ness', and Cicero translated it by the Latin 'qualitas', from 'qualis'. Language becomes a different thing for us altogether if we can make ourselves realize, can even make ourselves feel how every time the word quality is used, say upon a label in a shop window, that creative effort made by Plato comes into play again. Nor is the acquisition of such a feeling a waste of time; for once we have made it our own, it circulates like blood through the whole of the literature and life about us.[22]

I believe that the tremendous effort, "one of the most exhausting which man is called upon to exert" belongs to the phenomenology of the intimate relationship between language and consciousness and that this relationship involves the idea of participation.

In his little book, Speaker's Meaning, Barfield explores how our collective representations change over time. He distinguishes between lexical and speaker's meaning to show this process at work. Lexical meaning is the meaning of a word that we normally would accept as the meaning of the word. Speaker's meaning is a more individual variation of the lexical meaning. It is their interaction that advances culture, as in the example of Plato above.

Barfield goes to considerable length to show that the speaker does not invent a new shade of meaning, that is, the new variation of meaning does not arise from the speaker's subjectivity. To assume that it does is a fallacy based on current theory about the origin of language. Philology followed the findings of biology, particularly Darwin's *Origin of Species*, and so assumed that consciousness grew from a "mindless" state until one day an "exalted race of amateur poets" was born who could advance meaning by way of metaphors whose meaning originated in those poets' subjectivity.

If we reject this fallacy, then we are left with the conclusion that the meaning itself wishes to evolve and catches humans up in its evolution. Or, to put it another way, our collective representations evolve. As Barfield says, "the presence of living imagery is there in the language. It has objectivity to it. This may be called the wisdom of nature which is really what we are trying to say and avoid at the same time by the use of words like *instinct*." In other words, Barfield is describing a kind of inspiration that emerges from within the speaker and is felt to have the kind of autonomy that experiences of synchronicity do. Whereas ancient inspiration involved participation with the "inspiring power," felt to be outside oneself, now such experiences are felt to be from "within".

The close links between the phenomenon of synchronicity and that of inspiration are available to us today and demonstrate the possibility of final participation for our species. Barfield's successful reunion of philology and depth psychology enables us to draw on language that can help us extend our perceptions of phenomena sufficient to recognize moments of synchronicity or of inspiration. As individual speakers, we need to let one another know about these experiences for the sake of developing new collective representations. In this way our culture can slowly prepare for the evolutionary shift towards final participation.

To this end I want to conclude my own speaking by sharing another experience I had of participation as well as, sadly, its loss. I was sleeping on the couch in the living room as I sometimes do. The window opens to a forest. Beyond this are mountains in the east where the sun rises. On this particular morning:

As I was waking up, in a kind of in-between place with which I have since become more familiar, my eyes were still closed but I could see the room quite well as if they were open. I discovered LIGHT everywhere pervading my whole being. "My" being does not quite catch the experience. It would be more correct to say I saw the LIGHT OF BEING. Or even: The LIGHT OF BEING IS or, I, THE BEING OF LIGHT AM. There was no discernible distinction between the room, the light, and myself. Indeed these thoughts were not a part of it at all. Instead, GLORIOUS, LIGHT-FILLED BEING.

But then came thoughts: "Where is this coming from? I don't know of any light like this. Oh! It must be the light outside, the rising sun." With these thoughts, I felt a sudden separation, the glorious LIGHT withdrew to the outside, separated from me, and I became the receiver of the light. My eyes opened to the ordinary world I knew and I saw the sun rising in the mountains, out there so far away.

I felt a profound sadness. I had lost something of inestimable value and I had done it somehow with my own mind. But at least I gained the knowledge of what produces such loss and so maybe, next time . . .

End Notes

[1] Melville, H. *Moby Dick*. New York. Penguin, 1980, Ch. 74.

[2] Jung, C. G. *Nietzsche's Zarathustra: Notes on the Seminar Given in 1934-1939*. Princeton. Princeton University Press, 1988.

[3] Barfield, O. *Saving the Appearances*. London. Faber & Faber, 1962.

[4] Barfield, O. *History in English Words*. Hudson. Lindesfarne Press, 1967, 18.

[5] Campbell, J. *Primitive Mythology.* New York. Penguin, 1984, 9-10.

[6] Barfield, O. *Poetic Diction.* Hanover. Wesleyan Press, 1973, 138.

[7] Lockhart, R. *Words as Eggs: Psyche in Language and Clinic.* Dallas. Spring Publications, 1983, 102.

[8] Ibid. 95.

[9] Ibid. 98.

[10] AE. *The Candle of Vision.* New York. University Books, 1965.

[11] Barfield, O. *Origin of Language.* Spring Valley. St. George Pub., 1976, 7.

[12] Ibid. 29.

[13] Ibid. 7.

[14] Sugerman, S. *A Conversation with Owen Barfield.* Middletown. Wesleyan University Press, 1976, 14.

[15] Jung, C. G. *Modern Man in Search of a Soul.* New York. Harcourt, Brace and World Inc., 1933, 147.

[16] Barfield, O. *Speaker's Meaning.* Letchworth. Rudolph Steiner Press, 1967, 113.

[17] Barfield, Owen. *Saving the Appearances*, 35.

[18] Jung, C. G. *Modern Man in Search of a Soul*, 147.

[19] Jung, C. G. *Man and His Symbols.* New York. Anchor Books, 1964, 24.

[20] Barfield, O. *Saving the Appearances*, 41.

[21] Otto, Rudolph. *The Idea of the Holy.* New York. Oxford University Press, 1950.

[22] Barfield, O. *History in English Words*, 1967, 18-19.

TARNING

the process of manifesting possible futures

Owen Barfield coined the concept of tarning, adapting the word from the German *tarnung*: "The word *Tarnung* was, I believe, extensively used under the heel of the Nazi tyranny in Germany for the precautionary practice of hiding one meaning in another."[1]

Barfield needed this concept to name the process of advancing new meaning in culture through language. Dictionaries are an expression of congealed meanings, or norms, in language but these norms do change over time, as etymology teaches us. The concept of tarning gives us a means to examine these changes, through a microscope, as it were.

When a possible future is pressing forward into consciousness, as a new meaning, then the human participant in effect has something new to say but this new meaning must be said through already established words (dictionary meanings). It must be this way because speaking new meaning in a totally new word would be unintelligible to others. There must be some communication as well as expression, in order for others to grasp the new meaning that is suggested through the use of the old word. An example of tarning that borders on the unintelligible, i.e., is mostly expressive and least communicative is Lewis Carroll's Jabberwocky:

'Twas brillig, and the slithy toves
Did gyre and gimble in the wabe:
All mimsy were the borogoves,
And the mome raths outgrabe.[2]

In this case there does appear to be some tarning in which new meaning is meant through the use of established words, which, however, considerably "distorted", e.g. "slimy" becoming "slithy" etc., but when I read this famous passage I do at least get strange images of swamps and weird dancing.

Tarning is a process in which:

> Every man, certainly every original man, has something new to say, something new to mean. Yet if he wants to express that meaning (and it may be that it is only when he tries to express it, that he knows what he means) he must use language—a vehicle which presupposes that he must either mean what was meant before or talk nonsense!
>
> If therefore he would say anything really new, if that which was hitherto unconscious is to become conscious, he must resort to tarning. He must talk what is nonsense on the face of it, but in such a way that the recipient may have the new meaning suggested to him. This is the true importance of metaphor.[3]

In other words, Barfield has given us a concept so that we can begin to think the process of a possible future emerging into consciousness through individual participation, and thence into metaphorical language, which may be discerned as such by others. The new meaning thus begins its "descent" into manifestation and becoming, finally, "world."

Barfield gives a particularly compelling example of tarning in his beautiful "historical imagination" of Jesus' parable of the sower and its effect on his disciples. The nascent meaning of the Logos appearing "in earthly soil", i.e., in the hearts and minds of his listeners (at least for those who hath ears) was spoken *through* the well-established external meaning of sowing in the earth.[4]

Tarning is a concept that neatly conveys four conditions for the manifestation of possible futures, beginning with a nascent appearance within an individual who participates in its becoming. The individual then expresses/communicates to those others who "hath ears to hear". The listeners (who hath ears) must necessarily have the same seed of new meaning within them, too, i.e., the same possible future must be approaching them as well. Further manifestation than occurs as the new meaning sinks into habitual use, becoming in turn a perception or "world"—actuality!

A critical emphasis is needed here in discussing Barfield's concept of tarning: "If therefore he would say anything really new, if that which was hitherto unconscious is to become conscious, he must resort to tarning".[5] This crucial aspect of tarning points to the enormous creative effort by the individual to "find the right words" that will no longer mean what they usually mean, but instead will mean the new meaning. This cannot be said explicitly, but can only be suggested. This is the essence of tarning and the phenomenology of manifesting possible futures.

Barfield reminds us of the intimate and pervasive connection between tarning and language:

> Everywhere in language we seem to find that the process of tarning, or something very like it is or has been at work. We seem to owe all these tropes and metaphors embedded in language to the fact that somebody at some time had the wit to say one thing and mean another, and that somebody else had the wit to tumble to the new meaning, to detect the bouquet of a new wine emanating from the old bottle.[6]

Tracing back from a given congealed cultural form, or established meaning, or perceived aspect of the real world to the individual effort is difficult but not impossible, Shakespeare being an outstanding example of a known individual who infused our entire culture with 1700 fresh words, as well as many new phrases. If we succeed in doing so, we can get a microscopic glimpse of the "primal stuff", in the form of thinking or image that the individual participated, on the way to bringing the transformed matter into the world.

There are some modern examples where it is possible to not only trace back to the individual effort but to demonstrate all four conditions still at work in shaping the contours of reality today. These examples also demonstrate different scales in which the world and consciousness can transform.

Mandelbrot & the Fractal

If you look up "fragment" in the America Heritage Dictionary, you can go to the "root" *bhreg*, which is said to be the original sound-meaning from which a host of cognates spring. The root carries an image of breaking and one of the cognates mentioned is "fractal". To the uninformed reader this word, with its collective meaning of a geometrical shape in which self-similar patterns are found across scale, simply belongs with all its sibling words as if for all time. Yet its birth as a word can be traced to a specific time and to a specific individual:

> One wintry afternoon in 1975, aware of the parallel currents emerging in physics, preparing his first major work for publication in book form, Mandelbrot decided he needed a new name for his shapes, his dimensions, and his geometry. His son was home from school, and Mandelbrot found himself thumbing through the boy's Latin dictionary. He came across the Latin fractus, from the verb frangere, to break. The resonance of the main English cognates—fracture and fraction—seemed appropriate. Mandelbrot created the word … fractal.[7]

Such a tiny moment: two known words, "fracture" and "fragment", are joined to form a new word: "fractal".

This new word facilitated new meaning into the world. As Gleick reports, Mandelbrot had spent twenty years extending his perception into an aspect of reality (its "regular-irregularity") for which he yet had no word. He had to invent it to convey his new perception. Now the word and its meaning are widely accepted.

Those who follow Mandelbrot's pioneering work can like-wise extend their perceptions into reality through the agency of the concept he brought forward. Although the fractal nature of the world has not yet gained universal acceptance, (in the way that atoms have for example, or gravity, or geometric space), it now is in the public market of competing meanings, along with other conceptions of nature that are appearing.

Bernays & Public Relations

This is not a harmless process as we can see in the example of Edward Bernays. Ideas were swirling around the West during and after the First World War. Freud had discovered the unconscious and conceived it as a vessel of hidden desires that threaten the stability of the ego that seeks to conform to its environment. These desires are dangerous, animal-like, requiring defences. He later famously wrote Civilization and its Discontents in which he portrays civilization as the only bulwark against the Visigoth-like desires of the unconscious. Since these desires should never be released, civilized people are always in a state of necessary discontent.[8]Another idea sharpened into focus during the war and concerned the deliberate manipulation of "the masses" for purposes of war. Governments, in order to control public opinion, adopted propaganda to further its own cause. These two ideas, fermenting independently in the pool of available ideas, simply needed a fertile imagination to unite in what we may someday describe as an "unholy marriage". This fertile imagination belonged to Edward Bernays who was working for the American Government as a press agent during the war. His slogan: Make the World Safe for Democracy became a major player in the propaganda effort. He was also the nephew of Sigmund Freud.

After the war Bernays asked a simple question: Is it possible to manipulate the masses for purposes of *peace*? The two ideas flowed together into one and the field of Public Relations was born. Edward Bernays brought the ideas together under this new concept. His goal was "the conscious and intelligent manipulation of the organized habits and opinions of the masses …" His methodology was to stimulate unconscious desires in people and then extinguish those desires in a commercial product. The effect of this method is to make people into consuming, docile "happiness machines" while the "few" in power pursue their own political and economic ends.[9]

I felt the full extent of his effects on our culture when I was in New York in 2004. My wife and I were on the street near Times Square when a young man invited us to the David Letterman Show. We decided to go and witness this "archbishop of the inconsequential". We were not disappointed. In an advertising segment, he paired the horrors of Iraq with a product called Atomic Popcorn. The subliminal message is: "all your unconscious fears and anxieties can safely be extinguished in a bag of light fluffy candy whose explosion (pop!) cannot possibly hurt you." Public Relations at its finest!

We can witness the enormous cultural influence that

Edward Bernays' ideas have today. There are many eloquent critics who point out the excesses of misinformation that shape public opinion today but the phenomenon seems unstoppable. Any criticism is merely twisted into another aspect of the propaganda. As early as 1933, Bernays caught wind of the possibility of his ideas being taken up in a way that was less than wholesome. Goebbels, supreme architect of Nazi propaganda, had used Bernays' book Crystallizing Public Opinion as a basis for his own destructive campaign against the Jews of Germany. Bernays was shocked.[10] I wonder today if he would be proud or horrified at the level of sophistication attained by the Public Relations Industry and its role in shaping the Iraq War, for example. The Public Relations industry has become so bold, so confident of its own abilities, that it does not need to hide or disguise its theories, manipulations etc. I remember the movie in which a Hollywood director was hired by the CIA to "invent" a completely fictitious war that existed only on the TV sets of millions of Americans. It was brilliantly conceived and carried out.[11]

Whatever we may think of Public Relations and its determinative force in the world today, its possibility began in the imagination of one individual who, like Mandelbrot, accepted the union of two disparate ideas and chose to incarnate that union in a new concept, bringing forward new meaning and shaping the world accordingly.

As these and other examples show, for the first time in the history of our species, we are participating in the formation of possible futures on an unprecedented scale. In former times, only individual geniuses like Shakespeare rose to the level of participation in reality's underlying logic and its self-transformation. Today we seem to be in a collective uproar of more or less conscious participation in the transformation of consciousness and reality, as a multitude of art forms burst into the bewilderingly complex market of meanings. More and more individuals show a willingness to encounter the spontaneous weavings of the soul and then to make choices to incarnate this or that image of possible futures. We only need to glance at the plethora of "New Age" books in which the author claims that he or she is channeling the voices(s) of the spirit which is informing them and us of an imminent future reality.

C. G. Jung & the Jungian Unconscious

In 2009 a truly remarkable book was published: The Red Book, by C. G. Jung.[12] This long-awaited book shows the psychological process Jung underwent and endured over several years, culminating in the Jungian conception of the unconscious. He called this period of his life his confrontation with the unconscious.[13] However, The Red Book shows much more than the development of a conscious concept. It also shows us how a possible future manifests through the efforts and participation of one individual, Jung.

In Shamdasani's Introduction to The Red Book, he describes the beginnings of Jung's decades-long involvement (1912-1959) with The Red Book and the Black Books that preceded it:

> Up to this point, Jung had been an active thinker and had been averse to fantasy: 'as a form of thinking I held it to be impure, a sort of incestuous intercourse, thoroughly immoral from an intellectual viewpoint'. He now turned to

analyse his fantasies …

Jung picked up the brown notebook which he had set aside in 1902, and began writing in it … it occurred to him that he could write down his reflections in a sequence. He was "writing autobiographical material but not as an autobiography."[14]

Jung called his activity an experiment, an intentional procedure in which he "switched off consciousness", deliberately "evoking a fantasy in a waking state, and then entering it as into a drama". His aim was "to allow psychic contents to appear spontaneously. He recalled that beneath the threshold of consciousness, everything was animated. At times it was as if he heard something. At other times, he realized he was whispering to himself".

Shamadasani reports Jung's uncertainty during this period (1913) concerning the meaning and significance of his undertaking. This uncertainty lasted throughout his life, leading to much ambivalence concerning its publication. As late as 1959, two years before his death, Jung once again approached The Red Book in order to complete it, but broke off mid-sentence. He had previously suggested that "it and the Black Books be given to the library of the University of Basel with a restriction of 50 years, 80 years, or longer …"

Perhaps the most succinct expression of Jung's uncertainty concerning the nature of The Red Book, or his activities recorded therein, appears in dialogue form in his second Black Book. A voice informs him unambiguously that what he is doing is art—a claim that he vigorously disputes, making the counter-claim that what he is doing is nature. Only a portion of the long dialogue seems to be available at this time (2012) but has been source of serious discussion and speculation subsequently within the Jungian community.[15]

Shamdasani describes the overall content of The Red Book as a series of active imaginations together with Jung's attempt to understand their significance. He further describes the overall theme of the book as how "Jung regains his soul and overcomes the contemporary malaise of spiritual alienation". This is achieved through the "rebirth of a new image of God in his soul and developing a new worldview in the form of a psychological and theological cosmology".

Shamdasani's understanding of the content and theme of The Red Book finds resonance with Jung's own words as recorded in his well-known letter to Sir Herbert Read in 1960 in which he speaks of the "Great Dream" and identifies it with "the future and the picture of the new world."[16]

Lockhart comments that the emphasis here is not on "the ego's predicting the future—using dreams for power —but on man's conscious reflection and eros involvement in responding to the images bearing the incipient future in such a way as to participate *with* God in the birth of the manifest future".[17]

From this brief overview of Jung's conscious intentions in writing The Red Book we can see that Jung was actively involved in a psychological process that demanded *both* his understanding and participation in it. His understanding, as well as that of subsequent commentators, is of the birth within himself of a new reality, a birth which, as he later says, was "the material that burst forth from the unconscious, and at first swamped me. It was the *prima materia* for a lifetime's work".[18] Shamdasani shows how Jung indeed went on to develop and refine his understanding, producing a plethora of fresh and lasting contributions to our culture.

In this way we can see a semantic continuity between the content in The Red Book and Jung's subsequent life-long work as a psychologist of the soul. It appears that all subsequent auditors accept Jung's own position that the meaning of The Red Book is that of *"prima materia* for a lifetime's work". That is to say, we can successfully examine The Red Book to find the origin of Jung's later, more fully developed thought. In this way the understanding of future scholars or members of the Jungian community simply imitates Jung's own ideas about the meaning of The Red Book, carrying them further into manifestation, without questioning Jung's own understanding of the meaning of his activities recorded in The Red Book.[19]

A possible future has definitely manifested and flourished since Jung's time. We could call it the Jungian worldview which has touched the lives of many and produced a profusion of secondary literature and other cultural forms that simply would not have been possible without Jung's seminal ideas, all of which originates, as he says, in The Red Book.

The Jungian worldview holds that, within us, i.e., "in the unconscious", there may be found those precious soul qualities that modern life longs for, since the end of the metaphysical world, or, as Barfield says, the Aristotelian "mindscape":

> Our contemporary "mindscape" dates back roughly to the Scientific revolution … It was preceded by a very different mindscape, which had endured from some time in the first millennium BC to about the seventeenth century AD; and

which I will call "Aristotelianism"… this earlier mindscape was one which assumed an intercommunion between man (the microcosm) and nature (the macrocosm)…[20]

These soul qualities include interconnectedness, wisdom, and divinity in nature (imaginal depth), immediacy of appearance, numinosity, and autonomy of an intelligent *other-as-subject*—all those qualities that have disappeared from modern existence, as so many poets, artists, and philosophers have articulated, and as so many ordinary people sense today.

Within the Jungian community and to some extent beyond, particularly in the relatively new discipline of eco-psychology, Jung's historically new view of human beings (as carrying within themselves those soul qualities that once invested the world with meaning) has been taken up by others who "agreed" to see things the same way as Jung, and therefore, finally, to see the world that way:

(Jung's) main argument is that what we have lost, we have to find again. Even in this statement he concedes that the psychic connection to the cosmos has "sunk into the unconscious." That is why in dreams, he believes, we can still experience the ancient mystical at-one-ment with nature that is lost to our rational or waking mind.[21]

In this way, Jung's concept of the unconscious has entered the public market of meanings, competing, like the fractal, public relations, and many New Age messages, in the formation of a future reality the final form of which is as yet not known.

Voluntary Purpose & Spontaneous Impulse

It is clear that, in each of these modern examples, a new

concept or worldview has been produced to some degree through the creative efforts of individuals. And it is equally clear that others have to some degree agreed to see the world that way and, finally to see that kind of world. Whether and to what degree they each involve tarning, i.e., the process of possible futures and becoming manifest requires a still more microscopic examination. Tarning is "the concept of saying one thing and meaning another"—symbols, metaphors, and similes being the prime carriers of such speech.[22]

Barfield's example of the parables of Jesus demonstrates tarning at work in that Jesus had to say "A" in order to mean "B". In so doing, "B" *could* manifest through "A". There is no other way for this manifestation to happen. In so speaking, Jesus was not merely espousing a new worldview, one that he had consciously thought up and decided to deliver cryptically to his disciples.[23] Rather he and his disciples were participating in the emergence of a possible future emerging from "within" or spirit. This episode of tarning involved the momentous, historically new, and previously un-heard of, transformation of interiority (logos) from nature to man. There was no human "unconscious" previous to that time—"within-ness" or interiority was the interiority of nature, not the interiority of human beings. In the parables we can see the very process of transfer of interiority out of nature to man:

> The parable, then, was about the sowing of the world, the Logos, in earthly soil. It was an attempt to awaken his hearers to this realization that this seed was within their own hearts and minds, and no longer in nature or anywhere without.[24]

Barfield goes on to remind us that "transition" is a

"misleading word for the violent change in the whole direction of human consciousness which, in the last resort, this must involve". The violence done to Jesus is of course paradigmatic and thus raised to the highest value, but elsewhere Barfield gives us a stark picture of this "violent change", in reference to the possible abandonment of *our* current reality (what he and many others call Cartesianism) in favour of a new reality (as yet, of course, unknown):

> It might be thought that ... such a change could take place without any great upheaval. After all even in our Cartesian world quite a number of people seem to hold theories about the relation between man and nature which are incompatible with an absolute gulf between mind and matter ... but any forecast based on such considerations ... overlooks the extent to which Cartesianism has progressed from conscious to unconscious or "subliminal" conviction. "Materialism" ... means, not any materialistic philosophy ... but a mental habit of taking for granted, for all practical purposes and most theoretical ones, that the human psyche is intrinsically "alienated" from nature ... a habit so inveterate as to have entered into the meanings of a great many common words and thus to have been accepted as common sense itself. Materialism in this sense is not, for instance, incompatible with deep religious conviction.[25]

If tarning is at work then, we may expect to find, as well as the four conditions that I proposed above (which appear in Barfield's quote here, above), signs of resistance, even in the "hearers", i.e., those who hath ears. Barfield goes on to extend his picture of the consequences of such a "transition":

> Let us nevertheless suppose that the resistances are eventually overcome and try to imagine a second stage of transition. This surely must be a climate of extreme

depression amounting in many quarters to despair ... I am simply forced to envisage an epidemic of something like nervous breakdowns, with probably some suicides, within such solid fortresses of conformity as MIT or the London School of Economics and amongst their alumni.[26]

Interestingly, i.e., for the purposes of this book, in the same essay, "The Coming Trauma of Materialism", Barfield appeals to literature as the medium of choice to express any coming changes:

One way or another there is an opportunity here for a good writer in the genre of science fiction by a really imaginative writer, who should fill out in terms of concrete events and experiences the issues I have merely glance at ... If a society is really faced with startling changes and fairly imminent ones (and there is a good deal of evidence that ours is) it cannot be amiss for a few people here and there to be peering ahead, however inadequately, by way of preparation for them.[27]

While we may detect the echoes of tarning in the many rich metaphors of our language, the original act of tarning is an arduous and painstaking effort of an individual caught up in a process of meaning emerging into consciousness. The individual is thus, at first, mostly unconscious during this process of manifesting a possible future. Tarning happens to him or her as much as he or she makes it so. It is "an interpenetration ... of spontaneous impulse and voluntary purpose ... the potential works in them, even as the actual works on them!"[28]

From this deeper understanding of tarning, we are in a position to evaluate the modern examples I gave earlier. To what degree and in what way are they really examples of tarning?

Clearly in all three examples, the human author had a voluntary purpose: Mandelbrot had discovered a new geometry and wanted to name it; Bernays brought together Freud's concept of unconscious desire and the political idea of controlling public opinion, in order to invent a discipline; Jung wanted to "rescue Meaning", i.e., the lost spiritual treasures of the past, by positing an unconscious "within" us that is the new locus of such treasures.

We may think of these conscious efforts as "projects" —the task that the author intends to carry out in the course of their efforts. Tarning, or the manifestation of a possible future, should not be seen simply as the *project* of the author, because, as well as voluntary purpose, tarning involves "spontaneous impulse", i.e., a possible future is *emerging* into consciousness and the author is usually quite unconscious of this aspect.

Subsequent beneficiaries of these authors' efforts most often simply agree to see things the same way the author does, i.e., only in terms of the conscious project or voluntary effort, and then to see the world in that way, as I said previously.

Barfield addresses this crucial difference between conscious project and underlying, suggested meaning in his concept of "unresolved positivism". He notes that our current modern reality is that of positivism (Cartesianism) in which an unbridgeable gap is felt between mental experience and the objective world "out there". Many writers today are attempting to overcome this gap by turning our attention to the putative interconnectedness of nature, or the inherent divinity of life, or the consciousness of nature etc. The belief seems to be that, by thinking these already conscious thoughts, we *in fact* overcome the positivism that is our modern reality:

> Unresolved positivism occurs when that conviction, that imagination, that way of looking at mind or body remains in fact in a man's mind even though he may have in philosophical theory rejected or resolved it.[29]

A simple example may illustrate this. Much research has gone into the evolution of consciousness and here seems to be general agreement that ancient consciousness was fundamentally different from our own, modern consciousness. We sense that our forbears were "intertwined" with or participated with their world in a way that is lost to us. They must have therefore lived in a fundamentally different world, too. Yet, our dominant theory of evolution rests on the premise that the world has been the same world for all time (Uniformitarianism) *and* that same world we are talking about is that world corresponding to *our* modern consciousness. In other words, while we may *talk* of participatory consciousness and the real world that correspond to that form of consciousness, we simultaneously unthinkingly support and subscribe to a world that is completely independent of any consciousness.[30] As Barfield remarks ironically:

> … out of all the wide variety of collective representations [a term coined by Barfield to convey the inevitable polarity between consciousness and world] which are found even today over the face of the earth, and the still wider variety which history unrolls before us, God has chosen [so modern man assumes—my insert] for His delight the particular set shared by Western man in the last few centuries.[31]

Barfield's crucial distinction between voluntary effort and spontaneous impulse, along with his concept of unresolved positivism, approaches Wolfgang Giegerich's concept of the psychological difference. This concept points to the psychological fact that, while we may assert or claim certain viewpoints or worldviews (projects), our actual conduct in life is determined by the logical structure underpinning our consciousness. This underlying logical structure belongs to the time in which we are embedded historically, and we cannot change it, although we can relatively freely change our conscious worldviews.[32]

We can only "perceive" the possible future or emergent meaning that is emerging through these conscious projects by turning a *psychological* eye *to* the content, but not fixed *on* the content, so that the content becomes transparent to the suggested new meaning that is seeking manifestation into actuality.

In Mandelbrot's case of tarning, we can easily see the voluntary purpose in his seeking a word to name his geometry. We can also "see" the spontaneous impulse in his less conscious move of casually leafing through the Latin dictionary that his son left on the table. In so doing, Mandelbrot discovered the word "fractus", which springs from an etymological root meaning "to break". From the cognates, "fraction" and "fragment" he coined the new word, fractal. We are now in the position of asking what possible future reality may be "seen" emerging, as suggested by the actions taken by Mandelbrot in this act of tarning.

Mandelbrot coined the word "fractal" from words belonging to a group that carry meanings of breaking, broken-ness, rubble, breaching, crushing, etc. This suggests to me that this is a similar process to other attempts made today to heal what is felt to be broken, or unbridgeable, by using a contrivance. For example, we hear of words such as "psychosomatic", the "mind-body" problem, "psychophysical", "mind-brain", and so on. We can get a clearer picture of this attempt to overcome the unbridgeable when we take a closer look at what likely was in the back of Mandelbrot's mind as he was working towards a name for his geometry.

In developing his geometry of the irregular, such as a coastline, Mandelbrot realized that the length depended on "how close we are", or to put it another way, on the accuracy of the measuring instrument. The usual quantitative measurements (length, depth, thickness, etc.) failed to capture the essence of irregular shapes, since they all are relative to our distance from the object. Mandelbrot turned to the concept of dimension, which uses whole numbers to define space—three representing our normal space of solid bodies, for example. So, if we take a ball of string, its dimension changes as we get closer (far away—0-D, closer—3-D, closer still—1-D, etc.) Mandelbrot was concerned with how the dimension of the object could change abruptly between the whole numbers. To solve this geometrical problem Mandelbrot turned to fractions, which gave a "smooth transition". He could calculate the fractional dimensionality of his geometrical figures and that number proved constant over scale for a particular fractal representation of an irregular shape, like a coastline, or clouds—regular-irregularity.[33]

For our purposes we can see that the spontaneous impulse that was working in the background of his voluntary purpose concerned the overcoming of an unbridgeable difference (spatial dimension), just as neuroscience tries to overcome the gap between mind and body by coining "mind-brain", or as psychology attempts to overcome the split between self and world by inventing terms such as psychoid, or psychophysical, etc. The unbridgeable difference and its "overcoming" concerns our modern *reality* (called positivism, Cartesianism, etc.) and *possible futures* that are emerging, constituting new forms of consciousness that "overcome" positivism.

We can see the same background spontaneous impulse in Bernays' example of tarning. His voluntary purpose, as we have seen, was to establish the profession of Public Relations, which manipulates the unconscious desire of ordinary people for the sake of shaping public opinion (propaganda). Here we can see the same logic of difference working in the background of Bernays' thought, without which it would have been impossible to conceive Public Relations. Desire, for example, once belonged to the gods who subjected us to their will in order to fulfil *their* desires. I think of poor Paris in this regard. He was forced to choose the most beautiful among the three goddesses, who simply desired he do so. It was in the nature of a game for them. However, this game had deadly consequences for human beings, with the ten-year Trojan War that followed.

Desire then descended into human beings with the inevitable consequence of a new definition of man (*my* desires, *my* thoughts, *my* will etc.) but an invisible connection (participation) with the spiritual realm remained part of that definition until the 19th century when it was finally severed.[34]

With Bernays, we are able to see that desire is now a commodity, a thing that can be manipulated. The particular nature or quality of desire (fear, longing, erotic, etc.) is only important in so far as it influences the form of manipulation—e.g. what particular images are needed in the advertising etc. Desire no longer has any intrinsic worth, nor has any connection with a divine background to life. Similarly, all the intrinsic qualities that formerly defined individuals have been collapsed to their simple numerical difference as items side by side on a production line. This is a totally new definition of man that is working in the background of Bernays thought, as well as all those that followed. We can get a feel for this background by noting that when Bernays discovered that Goebbels was using his theory for his own purposes in Nazi Germany, he was shocked.[35] The only reason he *could* be shocked is that his voluntary purpose was dissociated in his mind from the spontaneous impulse working within the tarning.

Jung's efforts in writing The Red Book also involved his voluntary purpose (the content of The Red Book) and the spontaneous impulse working through the content as its only possible medium of expression (tarning). Only by carefully exploring the exact nature of Jung's participation in the creation of The Red Book can we begin to discern a possible future manifesting through the efforts of Jung, unbeknownst to him or, it seems, most subsequent auditors in the Jungian community.

It is striking to me that only one subsequent analyst has turned his and our attention to the content of The Red Book as a example of tarning, in which the content is understood as a medium of expression of the otherwise invisible spontaneous impulse (new meaning, possible future). Wolfgang Giegerich has shown that the text of The Red Book reveals a decades-long painful process in which Jung was drawn into installing, or fabricating (the underlying logical structure of) a new reality (possible future)—one that has little to do with his voluntary purpose of establishing the concept of the familiar Jungian unconscious.

Future commentators have not noticed this possible future until Wolfgang Giegerich, probably because of a lack of awareness of the process of tarning by which new meaning or new forms of reality come into existence. But this new reality has been imitated, and the four conditions necessary for the manifestation of a shared and real future have been met. This possible future, far from being continuous with the shared Jungian worldview developed from The Red Book by Jung and then others, is completely dissociated, yet remains determinative of real actions in the world, as we shall now see.

Jung's conscious conception of the unconscious is as I said based exclusively on his voluntary purpose (project) of The Red Book, with no attention given to the unconscious spontaneous impulse (underlying logic) that structures the content of The Red Book in the first place. It is only by giving attention to this underlying logic lying within the content of The Red Book that we are able to apperceive the possible future that *actually* comes into being through Jung's participation in making The Red Book.

Giegerich takes up this approach in his review of Shamdasani's book, Jung and the Making of Modern Psychology.[36] He asks:

> The question emerges for us how and why the unconscious did come to be conceived as a natural object (thereby opening up the project of rescuing god, or Meaning). The precondition was the great revolution from the

metaphysical [i.e. what Barfield calls the Aristotelan mindscape] to the positivisitc, scientistic stance at the beginning of the 19th century … the unconscious is the return … of the memory of and longing for metaphysics under the conditions of positivity.[37]

Giegerich's review of The Red Book appeared soon after in Spring Journal.[38] This review is the first and only one that examines the logical structure that underlies and *forms* the content that comprises The Red Book, when viewed psychologically. A certain preparation however, is needed in order to know how to approach this article and indeed The Red Book in order to grasp Giegerich's arguments and, finally, his conclusion.

When we dream and then wake up, the usual response on the part of the waking or empirical ego is to identify with the stance of the dream ego, basing one's understanding of the total dream on the particular stance of one element in the dream (the dream ego). Furthermore, many people base subsequent action in the world only on the dream ego's stance in the dream. However, It would be a fatal methodological mistake of the part of any psychologist of the soul to also take up the stance of the dream ego as the only one to consider when working with the dream, "[p]sychologically it is a grave mistake to privilege one element of a dream, fantasy, or psychic experience, for example the I, taking it literally by setting it up as a given existing outside the fantasy…"[39]

In other words, when we approach a dream or indeed The Red Book as a soul phenomenon, we must regard equally every aspect of the fantasies in order to understand them psychologically.

The results of doing just that are startling indeed and

Giegerich's long article is very persuasive in that it shows that "empirical" Jung i.e. Jung the dreamer identified solely with the *I* that appears within the fantasies, when he drew his conclusions about the nature of the unconscious. But if *we* pay equal attention to what Jung himself says as the internal other, i.e., as the *other* also appearing within the fantasy, a completely different picture emerges. I'll focus on just one aspect that demonstrates the nature of the possible future that pressed forward as a spontaneous impulse through Jung's voluntary effort (i.e. the content of The Red Book).

As Giegerich shows, Jung, from within the fantasies, repeatedly meets the figures appearing to him with a denial of their reality: within the fantasy where the *I* is merely one figure among others in the same fiction, Jung says, "surely you are symbols", "I am convinced that Izdubar is not at all real in the ordinary sense but a fantasy ..." As Giegerich says:

> Jung enters his fantasies with the categories of external reflection, namely with the distinction between fantasy and reality. Inside his fantasies, he views them from the outside and doubts the reality of their figures. It is as if a novel tried to pull the rug out from under its characters as only imagined, or as if we, while dreaming, turned around to the wild animal or to the murderous criminal chasing us and said to them, 'you are only symbols'.[40]

This means that Jung developed the capacity to enter his fantasies as the empirical I, able to view, from within his fantasies, *other figures as positive objects*! In this way he was able to simulate outer positive reality, *from within the fantasies*.

Jung unconsciously participated in fabricating a domain of "inner" reality that *simulates* outer modern reality (positivism, Cartesianism). The Jungian unconscious is *not* in reality a recapitulation of former ages in which reality has imaginal depth, but is a simulation of positivity, our modern structure of consciousness, the background logic of our existence over which we have no control. It is determinative!

Giegerich shows how Jung internalized the images of the natural or mental cosmos that formerly surrounded us, but did so under modern conditions of positivity, thereby constructing an "inner" that simulates modern empirical reality. It was a long, extraordinarily painful process, to the point of torture and madness, involving a kind of turning inside out of reality, or rather a turning outside in.[41]

In so doing, Jung, through the process of tarning, brought into being a reality that is a fabricated *simulation* of the outer empirical world of positivism. He unwittingly became a mouthpiece of this possible future and it has continued to manifest through the efforts of others, as well, independently of Jung.

At this time millions of people are logging on in order to participate in virtual or simulated reality (Second Life, Sim City, interactive games etc.), a product of our technological civilization. They enter a realm of image and interact with other images, *as* an image (avatar). Now we do this also on a daily basis when we dream or when we read a book. You could say that the empirical *I* becomes the fictional *I*, much like Alice is portrayed in Wonderland. So what is different with these technological worlds of simulation? When Alice drops into Wonderland, she leaves the categories of thought that belong to empirical reality behind and becomes fictional herself, evaluating this new reality within its own terms (remember her long conversations with the caterpillar and Humpty Dumpty for example). In fact when she does at the end employ an *empirical* category of thought, "O, you all are just a pack of cards!" she moves out of fictional reality back into empirical reality where she becomes a little girl once more. While she was inside the fiction, as a fictional figure, each character opens up to its own interiority and depth, its own truth.

In contrast, when we enter Second Life, for example, this does not happen. Instead, we enter as the *empirical I*, carrying with us all our empirical categories of thought. We know and do not forget that the avatar we meet on the street is a construction, like our own avatar, an "object", like empirical objects, only in the form of an image *positivized*. These images have no inner depth, or interiority. Any imaginal nature has been destroyed altogether. In other words we do not relate to a user's avatar in the way Alice relates to the imaginal figures of Wonderland. No one asks a Celtic warrior avatar about his initiation, his battles, his losses, his wisdom etc. Images are treated as empirical objects, related to by the empirical ego, *from within the fantasy*, with its empirical categories of thought. This is exactly analogous to lucid dreaming in which the fictional ego "wakes up" within the dream into its status as empirical ego and applies its categories of thought to what it then sees: "O, these are all just symbols or dream images. I can do anything I want. I'll try flying etc."

This is the psychology of simulated or fabricated reality! Fabricated reality *is* a reality—one that simulates positive reality *in the realm of images itself* (the imagination). Images are regarded with categories of thought that properly belong to empirical reality, and regarded as such from within imaginal reality itself.

When we make the distinction between the content (voluntary purpose) of The Red Book and the way its content is structured (the spontaneous impulse that informs the content), we can thus see that two dissociated conceptions of reality emerge in the Jungian project. The content speaks of the unconscious as the new, private domain of reality, which recapitulates the phenomenology of the public reality of former ages (immediacy, objectivity, autonomy, truth, epiphany, divinity, meaning, etc.) This conception is accepted by subsequent generations of people who agreed to see things the same way, leading to the establishment of cultural forms (Jungian Analysis and so on) that teach others to see things the same way, i.e., the Jungian "worldview" which now competes with other worldviews in the public market of meanings today.

A careful psychological analysis of the spontaneous impulse of The Red Book leads to a very different conception of reality, a fabricated reality that simulates our outer positivistic reality, within the world of image. Unbeknownst to Jung and the generations that followed, Jung participated in the formation of the logical structure that underlies what later came to be known as simulated reality, a reality that truly belongs to our modern technological age, giving rise, for example, to the possibility of television.[42] This reality is determinative of our modern existence, not merely a worldview, and as such may properly be called a possible future manifesting into actuality through the efforts of the man Jung. In this way we may see that The Red Book truly shows a process of tarning taking place.

It is particularly illuminating to turn to the mass media

today to find a "text" that completely confirms, demonstrates, and even applauds the logic of simulated reality, that same possible future that Jung brought into existence through his "confrontation with the unconscious" as recorded in The Red Book.

The 2009 smash hit movie Avatar points to a lost world of our past, a nostalgic longing for a natural world saturated with spiritual meaning. The native inhabitants live in perfect harmony with nature. Exploitative humans, who proceed to mine the planet for its mineral riches, destroying the lives of the innocent natives, as well as their habitat, colonize this world. The content of the movie appealed greatly to our current longing for former times when we supposedly had a much more intimate connection with a nature felt to be alive and conscious. The plot even proposes that a return to such a pristine existence is possible through the use of technology, in particular, avatars!

Today tens of millions of people are now online, *doing* what the movie represents so well with an astonishing acceptance of its ordinariness. The fact that millions on a daily basis are doing what the movie proposes as a possibility may account for the easy acceptance of the movie's premise and central symbol (Avatar!). Millions, maybe tens of millions now, are entering their own avatar in order to inhabit another world for as long as they like. However, if we turn a psychological eye to the "text" of the movie, i.e., to the logical structure underlying and permeating the content of the movie, another picture looms up behind. This is not a movie about a lost innocence. It is training manual for the West, urging us to go further in what we can already do—enter an avatar and go into, not nature, but cyberspace. Avatar is the common name known to millions of "gamers" who daily enter "Planet Pandora" and engage in the same impossible feats that are shown in the movie. The beautiful images have no correspondence at all with nature on earth, past or present, and are merely the scientific means (graphics, 3-D etc.) by which the modern ego is captivated and seduced into leaving earthly reality and entering cyberspace, perhaps forever, as our hero did. But we should note well: when he did succeed in becoming a Pandorian resident, his earthly body *died*!

This is no mere fantasy. Millions are doing it already. This movie simply acts as an openly seductive engine, in the best spirit of Public Relations, designed to encourage a particular "solution" to our loss of meaning and isolation. Our collective nostalgia for the past, a fancied innocence, and primordial oneness etc. is simply the "unconscious desire" that can be caught and manipulated towards other ends, as the public relations industry knows so well. For all those who think it is about primordial nature and rediscovering our interconnectedness, I would urge them to remember how our hero enters Pandora: he lies in a coffin and "dies" just as millions do when they log on. They die to the ordinary world and their bodies waste away as they spend twelve or sixteen hours online in cyberspace enjoying their freedom—freedom from ordinary reality which is becoming harder to bear as we witness the accelerating emptying out of meaning in the natural world!

Avatar is a movie spelling out the method and encouraging what millions really want to do—escape earthly reality altogether and enter cyberspace, at the cost of earthly life altogether. As determined by its logical structure or syntax, Avatar is decidedly *not* a movie showing us how to reclaim our interconnectedness and oneness with nature. Pandora is not a representation of nature at all. It is a true and accurate representation of what we are already building and investing billions of dollars in—cyberspace or virtual reality. Virtual reality *is* a reality indeed but *not* a natural one—it is a fabricated one! The entire engine of our modern technological society is now geared towards the invention of cyberspace into which we are now *openly* being invited. We are to inhabit it in exactly the way shown by the movie, leaving behind, as the movie also shows, a dead earth and a dead body.

This movie is only one example of cultural forms emerging in our times, which accurately reflect and strengthen the dissociation between the consciously held conception (Jung's "recovery of lost innocence") and the underlying logical structure of a possible future that is fast becoming a shared and real existence (fabricated or simulated reality). The Red Book thus provides us with a soul phenomenon ("dream" text) that beautifully exemplifies the four conditions I outlined above involved in the process of tarning. We can also describe the process as one in which the human mind participates in the self-transformation of the living logic that determines the next forms of reality. We are still in a great state of flux as I said earlier—many forms of reality seem to be "incarnating" at this time. I want to repeat the four conditions here:

1. The individual effort of participation with an aspect of possible futures;

2. The individual as mouthpiece of this future;

3. The willingness on the part of others to make a move towards seeing the world the same way the individual does;

4. The gradual congealing of that "way of seeing" into that way the world is seen, the world becoming "that way".

We can see that Jung's ordeal, as recorded in The Red Book, was such a participation in the logical life of the soul as it restructured itself as the logic of fabricated reality (Condition 1). He then propagated this new form of reality through teachings and writing albeit quite unconsciously (Condition 2). Jung believed he was promoting a quite different conception of the unconscious, as we have seen (his voluntary purpose or project). Others took up his conception and likewise propagated it further, also paying no attention to the underlying spontaneous impulse that was working its way further into manifestation *through* the conscious content. They thus also participated in the logic that gives rise to fabricated reality (Condition 3). Cultural forms that enact and reinforce that logic in actual deeds then sprung up and we are approaching that time when we are moving from this "way of seeing" to "the way the world appears" (Condition 4).

Tarning & Literature

We are living in a time when many possible futures are seeking manifestation through our more or less conscious participation in the process that Barfield names as tarning. The first forms that appear when reality is transforming, are artistic ones and today Contemporary Art demonstrates the multiplicity of possibilities:

> [C]ontemporary art is no longer one kind of art, nor does it have a limited set of shared qualities somewhat distinct from those of the art of past periods in the history of art yet fundamentally continuous with them. It does not presume inevitable historical development; it has no expectation that present confusion will eventually cohere into a style representative of this historical moment. Such art is multiple, internally differentiating, category-shifting, shape-changing, unpredictable (that is, diverse)—like contemporaneity itself.[43]

We have seen that C. G. Jung's The Red Book is a form of literature that Jung understood as *"writing autobiographical material but not as an autobiography."* We have further seen that Wolfgang Giegerich's analysis shows The Red Book to be a form of literature that involves tarning throughout, unbeknownst to Jung and, it seems, most other auditors of the book subsequent to its publication. There is no traditional genre of literature available to categorize such a book. As Giegerich demonstrates, The Red Book, as a record of tarning, shows how a possible future (in this case fabricated or simulated reality) may manifest *through* the voluntary purpose of the author, who may be quite unconscious of that process. Giegerich notes that, as recorded in The Red Book, Jung's experience of this manifestation of the spontaneous impulse, "… is a process which to a large extent has the nature of painful suffering and torment (up the point of near-madness) and is accordingly experienced as 'cruel', a very frequent word in The Red Book."[44]

Jung also describes his experience of this process of manifestation:

> I was so frequently wrought up that I had to do certain yoga exercises in order to hold my emotions in check. But

since it was my purpose to know what was going on within myself, I would do these exercises only until I had calmed myself enough to resume my work with the unconscious. As soon as I had the feeling that I was myself again, I abandoned this restraint upon the emotions and allowed the images and inner voices to speak afresh. …

To the extent I managed to translate the emotions into images—that is to say, to find the images which were concealed in the emotions—I was inwardly calmed and reassured. Had I left those images hidden in the emotions, I might have been torn to pieces by them.[45]

He reports that on one occasion:

… I tried to follow the same procedure, but it would not descend. I remained on the surface. Then I realized I had a conflict within myself about going down, but I could not make out what it was (the conflict then appeared to Jung as an image of two serpents fighting, one retired defeated and the fantasy then deepened) … I saw the snake approach me… the coils reached up to my heart. I realized as I struggled, that I had assumed the attitude of the Crucifixion. In the agony and the struggle, I sweated so profusely that the water flowed down on all sides of me … I felt my face had taken on the face of an animal of prey, a lion or a tiger.[46]

Jung later comments:

You cannot get conscious of these unconscious facts without giving yourself to them. If you can overcome your fear of the unconscious and let yourself down, then these facts take on a life of their own. You can be gripped by these ideas so that you really go mad, or nearly so. These images have so much reality that they recommend themselves, and so much extraordinary meaning that one is caught.[47]

These reports come subsequent to the writing of The

Red Book and as such are memories of Jung's experience. The following passage, however, occurs within The Red Book. A murdered child, and a woman standing by whose face is covered by a veil, confront Jung, within a vision. To his horror, the woman demands that he eat the liver of the child. He does so:

> I kneel down on the stone, cut off a piece of the liver and put it in my mouth. My gorge rises—tears burst from my eyes—cold sweat covers my brow—a dull sweet taste of blood—I swallow with desperate efforts—it is impossible —once again and once again—I almost faint—it is done. The horror has been accomplished.[48]

We are not here merely reading an imaginative account of what it would be like to eat the liver of a murdered little girl. As such we could compare this graphic description with many other, equally compelling, and perhaps even fascinating horror stories such as those by Edgar Allen Poe, or even Dante's journey through Inferno. We are instead witnessing a first-hand account of an actual experience of the empirical Jung, while in the realm of fantasy. Jung is not in the fantasy as a fictional *I* as Dante was in The Divine Comedy, but as the empirical *I*. The Red Book is analogous to reading a diary of a grotesque first-hand report of an actual act of cannibalism with the unheard-of twist that here, while Jung's reactions are empirical, the act is fictional!

There is a well-known widely defined form of literature called Magical Realism in which the process, which Jung went through in actuality, is explored *fictionally*. Magical Realism explores the impact fictional reality has on ordinary reality or, as C. S. Lewis puts it in reference to the books of Charles Williams, the effect of the "marvelous" invading the ordinary:

[In Williams' novels]: We meet, on the one hand, very ordinary modern people who talk the slang of our own day and who live in the suburbs. On the other hand we also meet the supernatural—ghosts, magicians, and archetypal beasts. The first thing to grasp is that this not a mixture of two literary kinds. That's what some readers suspect and resent. They acknowledge on the one hand straight fiction: the classical novel, as we know it from Fielding to Goldsworthy. They acknowledge on the other the pure fantasy which creates a world of its own cut off in a kind of ringed fence, from reality—books like Wind in the Willows … and they complain that Williams is asking them to skip to and fro from one to the other in the same work. But Williams is really writing a third kind of book which belongs to neither class and has a different value from either. He is writing that sort of book in which we begin by saying, "Let us suppose that this everyday world were at some one point invaded by the marvelous".[49]

Williams' books brilliantly describe the process of manifestation as purely fictional realities "invade" empirical reality:

She was where he had left her, but a dreadful change was coming over her. Her body was writhing into curves and knots where she lay, as if cramps convulsed her. Her mouth was open, but she could not scream; her hands were clutching at her twisted throat. In her wide eyes there was now no malice, only an agony, and gradually all her body and head were drawn up backwards from the floor by an invisible force, so that from the hips she remained rigidly upright and her legs lay stretched straight out behind her upon the ground, as if a serpent in human shape raised itself before him…

The face rounded out till it was perfectly smooth, with no hollows or depressions, and from her nostrils and her mouth something was thrusting out. In and out of her neck and hands another skin was forming, over or under her own—he could not distinguish which, but growing through it, here a coating, there an underveiling. Another and an inhuman tongue was flicking out over a human face … [50]

This is a graphic and vivid description quite analogous to the manifestation that Jung endured with *Leontocephalus*, which I will repeat here:

… I saw the snake approach me … the coils reached up to my heart. I realized as I struggled, that I had assumed the attitude of the Crucifixion. In the agony and the struggle, I sweated so profusely that the water flowed down on all sides of me … I felt my face had taken on the face of an animal of prey, a lion or a tiger.

Both Williams and Jung are describing a process in which a purely fictional figure manifests in the empirical human being, the crucial difference being that William's "empirical human being" is also fictional (a character in a story) whereas, for Jung it was happening to him, in empirical reality, *from within the fiction.*

The difference in the genres could also be expressed this way. The *character* in Williams' novel is going through the cruel transformation but it is unlikely that Williams the author went through it as well. Jung, however, did go through his own version of the experience that Williams' character went through, while he was recording the experience or shortly after:

I had no choice but to write everything down in the style selected by the unconscious itself. Sometimes it was as if I were hearing it with my ears, sometimes feeling it with my mouth, as if my tongue were formulating words; now and then I heard myself whispering aloud. Below the threshold of consciousness everything was seething with life.[51]

For Jung the fictional figures gained such a life that:

> At times he seemed to me quite real as if he [i.e. Philemon —one of many purely fictional figures that came to Jung's attention] were a living personality. I went walking up and down the garden with him, and to me he was what the Indians call a guru.[52]

We can even emphasise the difference further by noting that Williams and other authors of the broadly defined genre of Magical Realism would probably not have the concern that Jung had, as expressed by him:

> The more the images are realized, the more you will be gripped by them. When the images come to you and are not understood, you are in the society of the gods or, if you will, the lunatic society; you are no longer in human society, for you cannot express yourself. Only when you can say, "This image is so and so," only then do you remain in human society. Anybody could be caught by these things and lost in them—some throw the experience away saying it is all nonsense, and thereby losing their best value, for these are the creative images. Another may identify himself with the images and become a crank or a fool.[53]

Whereas C. S. Lewis referred to a genre of writing (Magical Realism) in which the marvelous invades the ordinary within the *fictional*, Jung's The Red Book is a record of this fictional invasion happening to him, the author, *empirically*:

> Around five o'clock in the afternoon on Sunday the front door bell began ringing frantically … there was no one in sight… The whole house was filled as if there were a crowd present, crammed full of spirits … then it all began to flow out of me and in the course of three evenings the thing was written [Septem Sermones—The Seven Sermons of the Dead]. As soon as I took up the pen, the whole ghostly assemblage evaporated. The room quieted and the

atmosphere cleared. The haunting was over … It was an unconscious constellation [i.e. invasion] … the numen of an archetype [the marvelous)] … The intellect, of course, would … like to write the whole thing off as a violation of the rules. But what a dreary world [the ordinary] it would be if the rules were not violated sometimes![54]

The new, as yet unnamed genre of literature that Jung seems to have inaugurated, involves *"writing autobiographical material but not as an autobiography,"* as I have said. It also is a process of tarning in which a new form of reality (possible future) manifests through the (mostly unconscious) efforts of the individual. If the four conditions I outlined above are fulfilled then that possible future may become our reality. We saw that this process of tarning was at work to some degree in the other examples I cited as well as in Jung's The Red Book.

The possible future that began to manifest through Jung's efforts, as recorded in The Red Book, is that of fabricated or simulated reality—that form of reality that subsequently has been reinforced in the realm of technology:

The purpose of [relating to purely fictional figure in terms of categories that belong to empirical reality] is to set it [i.e. fiction] as absolutely real in a naturalistic or positivistic (already reflected) sense. Fantasy has to simulate the character of hard-core reality for its fictions … much like the new 20th century technical medium of movies simulates reality so convincingly as to fool everyone.[55]

Tarning & Empirical Reality

There are many ways that our modern structure of consciousness can be characterized today. They all have in common the description of a split, dissociation, abyss, disjunction, or gap between different components of that structure, within the structure. Speaking in terms of an empirical-fictional dichotomy is therefore simply one other way to describe our modern consciousness. We all know the difference between fact and fiction in literature, for example, or non-fiction and fiction. Magical Realism is a genre of literature which portrays the fictional intruding into empirical life, as in the work of Charles Williams. Another compelling example is that of Stephen Marlowe who tells the story of the missing seven days of Edgar Allen Poe's life (i.e. no documented accounts of his whereabouts seem to be available) shortly before he died.[56] Marlowe's novel "melds fact and fantasy to transform fiction in a work of towering talent and illumination".[57]

Within this fictional account, Marlowe crafts a scene in which Poe is talking with the character of Dupin, a detective of Poe's own creation. It is not unusual of course for an author to engage their own figures of the imagination the same way we engage persons in empirical life. The disturbing element occurs when fictional Dupin begins to engage with people (a Dr. Moran and his wife) who are on the same side of reality as Poe, i.e., the empirical side (as such within this story). He sees them come into Poe's room and he and Poe talk afterwards about them. Later on, Dr. Moran is hurrying along a passageway when he hears footsteps pounding towards him. He sees no one. Something crashes him against a wall where he falls down. He sees an object on the ground and picks it up. He has a pair of spectacles, twisted and shattered. They belong, unbeknownst to Moran, to Dupin.[58]

From the examples of Williams and Marlowe, we can

see that such ingenious provocative and disturbing writing that goes by the name of Magical Realism, is only possible for a consciousness that is structured in a way that empirical reality is separated from fictional reality by a gulf.

This structure is a historical phenomenon and in order to understand this more fully, as well as to begin to comprehend the exact nature of tarning today, as the manifestation of possible futures, we need to imaginatively approach that historical time when empirical reality and fictional reality (modern terms with meanings that correspond only to our modern structure of consciousness) were not so separated.

It is well known that the scientific revolution inaugurated a new structure of consciousness and world in which the imagination was separated out from empirical reality according to the distinction between quality and quantity. Qualities of objects began to be understood as belonging to the subject while quantity belonged to the outer object.

We can turn to literature to get a feel for the way things were prior to that separation. Literature can take us back into former structures of consciousness that we have superseded today. When I read Nicolai Tolstoy's The Coming of the King, I am taken *into* that "time" in which (what we today would call) empirical and fictional realities were co-extensive to a degree that is impossible for us today. For the Celts at that time, it was simply the perceived world.[59]

Merlin and his companion Rufinus, a Roman tribune, are climbing a hill, engaging in animated conversation. As they climb, wild nature begins to encroach and civilized life fades in the distance.

> The air was raw and chilly, and cold had arisen upon a wind blowing the full length of the world from the hard unyielding planets set in the void above Dinleu Gurygon. The rough shoulder of the hill against which I leaned felt icy cold, and icy cold was I becoming myself … Rufinus was speaking, but I could feel the draw and power of the hill exerted upon me, and his words became faint and distant. Other sounds were replacing those of his broken Ladin speech. A nightjar, twisting silently in the night sky above us, uttered a guttural "churr, churr" from his great gaping mouth; like the tribune, he was newly come from Africa, and like the tribune his voice was harsh and broken. From all about me in the heather and upon the rocks came a rustling and squeaking and grunting … I heard bats squeaking in the rimy dark and felt faint breeze upon my face from the wings of blundering moths. The cold had become yet more bitter: cold, cold, cold. I felt as if I were frozen into the hard ground, like the exposed outcrop against which I leaned for support. The owl's discordant shriek heralded the rising of a night mist, a vapor from each hollow, an encircling gray hood about the hilltop. I did not doubt that it was the mist of Gwyn mab Nud, smoky unguent of the Witches of Annufn, a shaggy mantle over the land …

> I was wedged in the belly of the hill, my body stiff, cold, and inert. Before me, cross-legged upon a mound, sat a huge skin-clad herdsman, beside him a curly-haired mastiff bigger than a stallion of nine winters. Its breath was such that it would consume dead wood and yellowed tufts of grass upon the open Plain of Powys beneath. In his hand the great swart figure bore an iron club that would be a burden for two men to carry.[60]

Here we can see a seamless transition from ordinary reality to "the marvelous", as C. S. Lewis puts it. No intrusion, no invasion, no penetration! Ordinary reality simply recedes and what *we* might call fictional reality assumes ascendancy.

The spiritual tradition that Tolstoy's Merlin has mastered reaches back at least to the time of Parmenides. The central practice of initiates is that of the *Iatromantis*, or *Phôlarchos*, a practice of incubation that opened one up to spiritual reality. The practice simply involved crawling into a lair and "collapsing" or becoming still, while staying awake. Spiritual reality or simply Reality, is simply there, waiting for us. Merlin entered this state and found the mythic Herdsman already there waiting for him.[61]

As we know, that mythic world has come to an end and we may look for literary works, like Tolstoy's novel, that can take us into an experience of that world, saturated as it was with living meaning, at the "moment" of its ending. Cervantes' Don Quixote is such a book. It tells a story of a man for whom the imaginal richness of the world is still alive, while all around him, others have left that world and now inhabit our modern empirical world. Here is a scene where Don Quixote ("The Knight of the Rueful Countenance") is on an adventure with his servant ("squire"):

> At this point they came in sight of thirty forty windmills that there are on plain, and as soon as Don Quixote saw them he said to his squire, "Fortune is arranging matters for us better than we could have shaped our desires ourselves, for look there, friend Sancho Panza, where thirty or more monstrous giants present themselves, all of whom I mean to engage in battle and slay, and with whose spoils we shall begin to make our fortunes; for this is righteous warfare, and it is God's good service to sweep so evil a breed from off the face of the earth."

"What giants?" said Sancho Panza.

"Those thou seest there," answered his master, "with the long arms, and some have them nearly two leagues long."

"Look, your worship," said Sancho; "what we see there are not giants but windmills, and what seem to be their arms are the sails that turned by the wind make the millstone go."

"It is easy to see," replied Don Quixote, "that thou art not used to this business of adventures; those are giants; and if thou art afraid, away with thee out of this and betake thyself to prayer while I engage them in fierce and unequal combat."[62]

The imaginal world and the world that came into being with the scientific revolution, bringing with it a division between empirical world (the now real world) and the imaginal world (now downgraded to fiction) can thus be seen to be fundamentally different. Owen Barfield has beautifully captured this difference:

If, with the help of some time-machine working in reverse, a man of the Middle Ages could be suddenly transported into the skin of a man of the twentieth century, seeing through our eyes and with our 'figuration' the objects we see, I think he would feel like a child who looks for the first time at a photograph through the ingenious magic of a stereoscope. 'Oh!' he would say, 'look how they stand out!' We must not forget that in his time perspective had not yet been discovered, nor underrate the significance of this … Before the scientific revolution the world was more like a garment men wore about them than a stage on which they moved. In such a world the convention of perspective was unnecessary. To such a world other conventions of visual reproduction, such as the nimbus and the halo, were as appropriate as to ours they are not. It was as if the observers were themselves in the picture. Compared with us, they felt themselves and the objects around them and the words that expressed those objects, immersed together in something like a clear lake of-what shall we say? —of 'meaning'.[63]

Empirical reality is now privileged as *reality* and the former *imaginal* reality, as described above, and by Barfield, is now downgraded to fiction, a lesser reality, one that does not carry the same conviction of reality in the way that empirical reality does.[64]

With this clear demarcation in place, we are now in a position to return to the genre of Magical Realism, and Jung's The Red Book, and the astonishing soul movement portrayed as fictional reality bursting into, or invading, empirical reality.

Wolfgang Giegerich brings our attention to a compelling and popular icon of the early 20th century:

This famous poster by James Montgomery Flagg:

… shows a man dressed as Uncle Sam who points with his finger directly at the viewer saying, "I want YOU". Something extraordinary is happening here … The [fictional] person … breaks out of his containment within the fictional or imaginal world of the picture into the literal "external" [empirical] reality where the flesh-and-blood viewers live.[65]

Giegerich goes on to remind us that this instance of penetration by the fictional into empirical reality is itself fictional, i.e., not literally so:

But the poster of Uncle Sam is and remains a poster, an image. The Uncle Sam represented there does not in fact step out of the picture to us, the audience. He only appears to do so as long as we for our part look at the poster naturally, imaginally: are seduced into its aura. The busting of the image occurs in the image and as image.[66]

There are modern forms of theatre and performance art in which a more literal penetration into empirical reality is taking place. The audience is no longer seduced by the art *into* the reality of the play but is instead often addressed directly by the characters that even interact physically with the audience. Jung's descriptions of his own experiences, as recorded in The Red Book, show a similar process in which purely fictional figures impress *their* reality (which has historically been downgraded to a status of "not real") on the empirical Jung with great convincing power.

While, as I said, the genre of Magical Realism shows the penetration of fictional reality into empirical reality *within* the fictional form (as the Uncle Sam poster does), it seems to me that modern performance or participatory art, as well as Jung's The Red Book, are showing a further development in this movement. [67]

I would suggest that works such as Charles Williams are of the order of an *intuition* of a soul movement that is a development from the centuries long split between empirical reality and fictional reality. This historical split, also a determinative soul movement, has the consequence of privileging "outer" reality, the reality of surfaces, i.e., empiricism, and, at the same time, downgrading "inner" reality to what we now call fiction, or the imagination, to a status of "unreal".

I further suggest that the soul is engaging in a movement to transform this relationship between empirical reality and fictional reality. This soul movement is a modern form of tarning in which a possible future is manifesting through the efforts of individuals such as C. G. Jung.

The immense difficulty in comprehending this movement can be seen in Jung's efforts to comprehend what was happening to him. As I noted above, Wolfgang Giegerich's analysis of The Red Book shows that the possible future manifesting through C. G. Jung is a fabricated reality, a *simulated* empirical reality. I believe this conception, while certainly being a step along the way, as it were, needs refinement in order to fully comprehend this next soul movement that seems to be transforming the relationship between empirical reality and fictional reality. The intrusion of fictional reality into Jung's empirical life is simply an exemplary instance of what I believe to be a growing phenomenon throughout the world today.[68]

End Notes

[1] Barfield O. *The Rediscovery of Meaning*. San Rafael. The Barfield Press, 1977, 55 ff.

[2] Carroll, L. *Alice's Adventures in Wonderland*. Eire. Evertype, 2008.

[3] Barfield O. *The Rediscovery of Meaning*, 68.

[4] Barfield, O. *Saving the Appearances*. London. Faber & Faber, 1962, 178 ff.

[5] Ibid.

[6] Barfield O. *Rediscovery of Meaning*, 57.

[7] Gleick, J. *Chaos: The Amazing Science of the Unpredictable*. London. Vintage, 1997, 98.

[8] Freud, S. *Civilization and its Discontents*. (J. Strachey, Ed., & J. Strachey, Trans.) New York. Norton, 1961.

[9] Bernays, E. L. *Propaganda*. NY. Horace Liveright, 1928, 9.

[10] Bernays, E. L. *Biography of an Idea: Memoirs of a Public Relations Counsel*. New York. Simon and Schuster,1965.

[11] *Wag the Dog*. Starring Dustin Hoffman and Robert de Niro, 1997.

[12] Jung, C. G. *The Red Book*. (S. Shamdasani, Ed., S. Shamdasani, M. Kyburz, & J. Peck, Trans.) New York. W.W. and Norton & Company, 2009.

[13] Jung, C. G. *Memories, Dreams, Reflections*. New York. Random House, 1963, 170ff.

[14] All the following quotes from Shamdasani appear in the Introduction to *The Red Book*, 193-221.

[15] See my article: "The Red Book, Jung's Hidden Legacy" reproduced in my book, *Oblivion of Being*. CreateSpace, 2015.

[16] *C. G. Jung Letters:Vols. 2 (1951-1960)*. (G. A. Adler, Ed., & R. F. Hull, Trs.) London: Routledge and Kegan Paul, 1975, 586.

[17] Lockhart, R. A. Psyche Speaks, Wilmette. Chiron, 1987, 115.

[18] Jung, C. G. *Memories, Dreams, Reflections.* New York. Random House, 1963, 199.

[19] An outstanding exception is the work of Wolfgang Giegerich: Giegerich, W. "Liber Novis, that is, The New Bible, A First Analysis of C. G. Jung's Red Book". *Spring 83*, 2010, 361-413.

[20] Barfield O. *The Rediscovery of Meaning*, 217.

[21] Tacey, D. "Ecopsychology and the Sacred: The Psychological Basis of the Environmental Crisis"in *Spring 83*. 2010, 329-353.

[22] Barfield O. *The Rediscovery of Meaning*, 55.

[23] As Barfield says "... and it may be that it is only when he tries to express it, that he knows what he means." See his quote on *tarning* above.

[24] Barfield O. *Saving the Appearances*, 179.

[25] Barfield O. *Rediscovery of Meaning*, 218.

[26] Ibid. 228.

[27] Ibid. 229.

[28] Coleridge as quoted in Barfield O. *Speaker's Meaning*, 82.

[29] Sugerman, S. (Ed.) *Evolution of Consciousness: Studies in Polarity.* Middletown: Wesleyan University Press. 1976, 13.

[30] Uniformitarianism is the unprovable hypothesis proposed by Sir Charles Lyell that the laws of physics have been the same for all time. It is the basis of carbon dating, for example (the relative amount of carbon isotope being constant throughout time). Today we recognize that the world and our consciousness are somehow dependent on each other while simultaneously holding the view that the world is totally independent of our perceptions.

[31] Barfield O. *Saving the Appearances*, 38.

32 Giegerich's concept of the psychological difference is critical to understanding the complex nature of our modern consciousness. For a fuller discussion, see Giegerich, W. *The Soul's Logical Life.* Frankfurt. Peter Lang, 2001.

33 Gleick, J. *Chaos*, 97 ff.

34 Tillyard, E. *The Elizabethan World Picture: A Study of the Idea of Order in the age of Shakespeare.* New York. Vintage Books, 1942.

35 Bernays, E. L. *Biography of an Idea.*

36 Shamdasani, S. *Jung and the Making of Modern Psychology.* Cambridge: Cambridge University Press. 2003.

37 Giegerich,W. "After Shamdasani". *Spring 71*, 2004, 209.

38 Giegerich, W. *Liber Novis, that is, The New Bible.*

39 Ibid. 372.

40 Ibid. 402.

41 Giegerich, W. *Liber Novis, that is, The New Bible.*

42 Giegerich, W. *Technology and the Soul.*

43 Smith, T. *Contemporary Art: World Currents.* London. Laurence King Publishing. 2011, 9.

44 Giegerich, W. *Liber Novis, that is, The New Bible*, 391-392.

45 Jung, C. G. *Memories, Dreams, Reflections*, 177.

46 Jung, C. G. *Analytical Psychology: Notes on the Seminar Given in 1925.* (W. McGuire, Ed.) Princeton. Princeton University Press, 1989, 96-97.

47 Ibid.

48 Jung, C. G. *The Red Book,* 290.

49 *C. S. Lewis Lectures on the Novels of Charles Williams.* YouTube: https://www.youtube.com/watch?v=Z5w134gYz04

[50] Williams, C. *The Place of the Lion.* Vancouver. Regent College Publishing, 2003,170.

[51] Jung, *Memories, Dreams, Reflections*, 178.

[52] Ibid, 183.

[53] Jung, *Analytical Psychology*, 99.

[54] Jung, *Memories, Dreams, Reflections*, 190-191.

[55] Giegerich, W. *Liber Novis*, 403.

[56] Marlowe, S. *The Lighthouse at the End of the World.* New York. Plume, 1996.

[57] Ibid. Back Cover.

[58] Ibid. 323.

[59] Tolstoy, N. *The Coming of the King.* NY. Bantam Books. 1989.

[60] Ibid. 254 ff.

[61] Kingsley, P. *In the Dark Places of Wisdom.* London. Duckworth. 2001, 108 ff.

[62] de Cervantes, M. *Don Quixote*. (J. Ormsby, Trans.) Project Gutenberg, 1997. Retrieved 11/23/2012, from http://archive.org/stream/donquixote00996gut/old/1donq10.txt

[63] Barfield, O. *Saving the Appearances*, 94.

[64] For a fuller discussion of the archetypal basis of the division between empirical reality and fictional reality, see Giegerich, W. "The Rocket and the Launching Base", 2007.

[65] Ibid. 121.

[66] Ibid. 133.

[67] See my review of the Academy award winning movie for 2015, Birdman, for a fuller discussion of this provocative art form: https://independent.academia.edu/WoodcockJohn

68 See my essay, "The Red Book: Jung's Hidden Legacy." First published in Thomas Arzt (Hrsg.): *Das Rote Buch. C. G. Jungs Reise zum* "anderen Pol der Welt" Studien zur Analytischen Psychologie, Bd. 5, Königshausen & Neumann, Würzburg, Germany, 2015 and reproduced in my book, *Oblivion of Being*. Createspace, 2015.

ABOUT the author

I hold a doctorate in Consciousness Studies (1999). My thesis concerns the theme of "the end of the world", based on my own personal experiences lasting twenty years. At first it seemed to me that I was undergoing a purely personal psychological crisis but over time I discovered that I was also participating in the historical process of a transformation of the soul, as reflected in the enormous, even apocalyptic, changes occurring in our culture. During this difficult period of my life, I wrote two books: Living in Uncertainty Living with Spirit and Poems of Making, Poems of Death.

My next three books, Mouthpiece, The Imperative, and Hearing Voices, explore the meaning of "the end of the world" more fully. My subsequent books, including Animal Soul and Manifesting Possible Futures, establish a firm theoretical ground for the claim that the soul is urging us towards the development of new inner capacities that can help us face the uncertainty of modern life and, as well, address the unknown future.

My book, Overcoming Solidity, continues this exploration in terms of our current structure of consciousness and its correlative world of empirical reality. Making New Worlds begins the work of articulating the art form that is emerging in response the soul's intention to incarnate in the real world. I develop this theme more fully in The Coming Guest and the New Art Form. I have also written an unusual book, UR-image, which tells a story of four friends whose lives are interrupted by an intrusion of four possible futures, while Oblivion of Being is a story of three friends caught up in a transformation of being.

I currently live with my wife Anita in Sydney, where I teach, write, and consult with others concerning their own journey through the present "apocalypse of the interior", as it has been called, in my capacity as a practicing Jungian psychotherapist. Anita and I also work with couples in a therapeutic setting.

Contact: jcw@johnwoodcock.com.au